Ellington Middle School
Library Media Center

Lucille Ball

Ellington Middle School
Library Media Center

These and other titles are included in The Importance Of biography series:

Maya Angelou
Louis Armstrong
James Baldwin
Lucille Ball
The Beatles
Alexander Graham Bell
Napoleon Bonaparte
Julius Caesar
Rachel Carson
Charlie Chaplin
Charlemagne
Winston Churchill
Christopher Columbus
James Dean
Charles Dickens
Emily Dickinson
Walt Disney
Queen Elizabeth I
F. Scott Fitzgerald
Anne Frank
Benjamin Franklin
Mohandas Gandhi
John Glenn
Jane Goodall
Martha Graham
Lorraine Hansberry
Stephen Hawking
Ernest Hemingway
Adolf Hitler
Harry Houdini
Thomas Jefferson

Mother Jones
John F. Kennedy
Martin Luther King Jr.
Bruce Lee
John Lennon
Joe Louis
Douglas MacArthur
Thurgood Marshall
Margaret Mead
Golda Meir
John Muir
Richard M. Nixon
Pablo Picasso
Edgar Allan Poe
Elvis Presley
Eleanor Roosevelt
Franklin D. Roosevelt
Jonas Salk
Margaret Sanger
Oskar Schindler
Dr. Seuss
Frank Sinatra
William Shakespeare
Tecumseh
Mother Teresa
Jim Thorpe
Queen Victoria
Pancho Villa
Leonardo da Vinci
Simon Weisenthal

Lucille Ball

by Adam Woog

Lucent Books, 10911 Technology Place, San Diego, CA 92127

For Natalie Lucille Jennings Quinn,
born August 2, 2001

Library of Congress Cataloging-in-Publication Data

Woog, Adam, 1953–
    Lucille Ball / by Adam Woog.
        p. c.m. — (The importance of)
Includes bibliographical references and index.
Summary: Profiles the life and work of Lucille Ball, discussing her youth, movies, television, romances, marriage, divorce, achievements as a businesswoman, and legacy.
    ISBN 1-56006-746-2 (hardback : alk. paper)
    1. Ball, Lucille, 1911– —Juvenile literature. 2. Entertainers—United States—Biography—Juvenile literature. [1. Ball, Lucille, 1911– 2. Entertainers.] I. Title. II. Series.
    PN2287.B16 W66 2002
    791.45′028′092—dc21

2001004231

Copyright 2002 by Lucent Books, Inc., an imprint of The Gale Group, 10911 Technology Place, San Diego, California 92127

Printed in the U.S.A.

Contents

Foreword

THE IMPORTANCE OF biography series deals with individuals who have made a unique contribution to history. The editors of the series have deliberately chosen to cast a wide net and include people from all fields of endeavor. Individuals from politics, music, art, literature, philosophy, science, sports, and religion are all represented. In addition, the editors did not restrict the series to individuals whose accomplishments have helped change the course of history. Of necessity, this criterion would have eliminated many whose contribution was great, though limited. Charles Darwin, for example, was responsible for radically altering the scientific view of the natural history of the world. His achievements continue to impact the study of science today. Others, such as Chief Joseph of the Nez Percé, played a pivotal role in the history of their own people. While Joseph's influence does not extend much beyond the Nez Percé, his nonviolent resistance to white expansion and his continuing role in protecting his tribe and his homeland remain an inspiration to all.

These biographies are more than factual chronicles. Each volume attempts to emphasize an individual's contributions both in his or her own time and for posterity. For example, the voyages of Christopher Columbus opened the way to European colonization of the New World. Unquestionably, his encounter with the New World brought monumental changes to both Europe and the Americas in his day. Today, however, the broader impact of Columbus's voyages is being critically scrutinized. *Christopher Columbus,* as well as every biography in The Importance Of series, includes and evaluates the most recent scholarship available on each subject.

Each author includes a wide variety of primary and secondary source quotations to document and substantiate his or her work. All quotes are footnoted to show readers exactly how and where biographers derive their information, as well as provide stepping stones to further research. These quotations enliven the text by giving readers eyewitness views of the life and times of each individual covered in The Importance Of series.

Finally, each volume is enhanced by photographs, bibliographies, chronologies, and comprehensive indexes. For both the casual reader and the student engaged in research, The Importance Of biographies will be a fascinating adventure into the lives of people who have helped shape humanity's past and present, and who will continue to shape its future.

IMPORTANT DATES IN THE LIFE OF LUCILLE BALL

1940
Meets Desi Arnaz on the set of *Too Many Girls*, marries him later that year.

1948
Stars in hit radio series *M_ Favorite Husband*.

1933
Travels to Hollywood for a bit part in her first movie, signs with Metro-Goldwyn-Meyer Studios (MGM) as contract player.

1910	1920	1930	1940	1950

1911
Lucille Ball is born in Jamestown, New York, on August 6.

1934
Signs with Columbia Studios, then RKO Studios.

1950
Gets approval from CBS-TV to create a new show, *I Love Lucy*; forms Desilu Productions with Arnaz.

1926
Enters drama school in New York City.

1937
Appears in *Stage Door*, her highest billing and best vehicle to date.

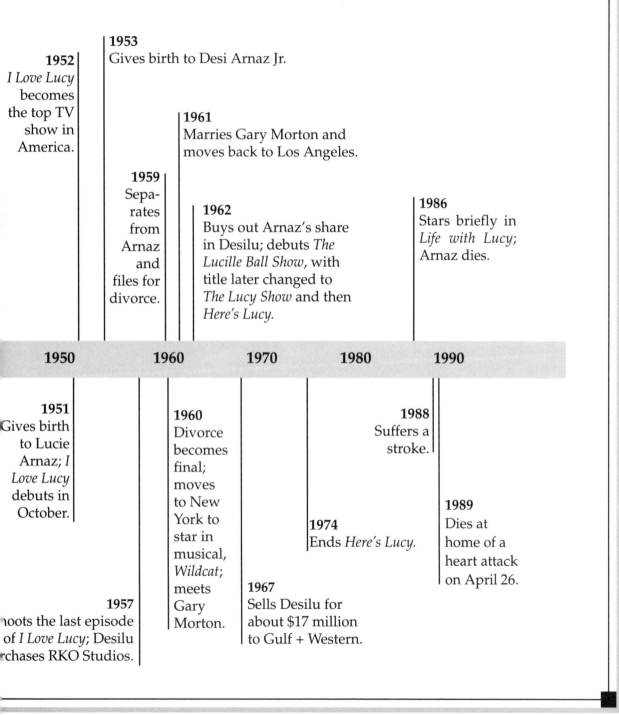

1952
I Love Lucy becomes the top TV show in America.

1953
Gives birth to Desi Arnaz Jr.

1961
Marries Gary Morton and moves back to Los Angeles.

1959
Separates from Arnaz and files for divorce.

1962
Buys out Arnaz's share in Desilu; debuts *The Lucille Ball Show*, with title later changed to *The Lucy Show* and then *Here's Lucy.*

1986
Stars briefly in *Life with Lucy*; Arnaz dies.

1950 **1960** **1970** **1980** **1990**

1951
Gives birth to Lucie Arnaz; *I Love Lucy* debuts in October.

1960
Divorce becomes final; moves to New York to star in musical, *Wildcat*; meets Gary Morton.

1988
Suffers a stroke.

1974
Ends *Here's Lucy.*

1989
Dies at home of a heart attack on April 26.

1967
Sells Desilu for about $17 million to Gulf + Western.

1957
Shoots the last episode of *I Love Lucy*; Desilu purchases RKO Studios.

The First Lady of Television

"I love Lucy. Everybody loves Lucy."
—comedian George Burns

Lucille Ball was the funniest, most renowned redhead who ever appeared on television. Never mind that Ball's hair was naturally a chestnut brown or that its color could not be seen on the black-and-white TV screens of the 1950s, when she ruled the airwaves. Ball's hair was her most immediately identifiable trademark, and she will forever be remembered as "that wacky redhead."

Ball was memorable, of course, for much more than just the tint of her hair. In the 1950s she was the world's best-known female comedian, and in the decades since, her fame has barely diminished. Because her programs have remained in syndication, Ball's comedy continues to live on into the present and attract new fans. Her trademark style—marked by an agile physicality, expressive face, and gutsy determination—has been the model for new generations of female comedians.

Furthermore, Ball was the first female to head a major Hollywood studio and to control virtually every aspect of the production of her work. This facet of Ball's life paved the way for women who have since risen to executive positions in the entertainment world, as well as female performers who direct their own production companies.

In addition to producing a comedic style that was wildly popular in the 1950s and continues to influence performers today, Lucille Ball also owned and ran her own studio, Desilu Productions.

NATIONAL DEVOTION

"Such national devotion to one show can never happen again; there are too many shows, on many more channels, now. But in 1951–52, our show changed the Monday-night habits of America. Between nine and nine-thirty, taxis disappeared from the streets of New York. Marshall Fields department store in Chicago hung up a sign: 'We love Lucy too, so from now on we'll be open Thursday nights instead of Monday.' Telephone calls across the nation dropped sharply during that half hour, as well as the water flush rate, as whole families sat glued to their seats."

TV SUPERSTAR

By the end of the 1940s, Ball was a reasonably well-known actress in the movies and on radio, but she was not hugely famous. Within a short period early in the next decade, however, Ball had become a genuine superstar.

The transition came about because she and her husband, Cuban-born bandleader and actor Desi Arnaz, took a chance. They created a show, starring themselves and loosely based on their real lives, for a new and largely untested medium—television.

It proved to be gold. *I Love Lucy* immediately shot to the top of the ratings. Ball rocketed to fame as America's biggest female TV star, one of the most recognized celebrities in Hollywood, and probably the world's top female comic in any field. Her gift for physical comedy, largely untapped until then, had found its perfect home.

For the next six seasons, *I Love Lucy* totally dominated American television. Dubbed into other languages, *Lucy* was also a smash hit around the world. It was so popular that department stores, churches, and other organizations had to alter their schedules. They wanted to accommodate the millions of people who refused to miss their Monday-night appointments with Lucy.

Because her shows remain immensely popular as reruns, it is likely that no television entertainer has ever enjoyed such long-term and widespread renown as Lucille Ball. According to her daughter, Lucie Arnaz, *I Love Lucy* is "simply the most watched TV show in history."[1]

THE STAR OF THE SHOW

The program was memorable, first and foremost, because Ball was funny, and it always revolved around that single fact. Referring to the rest of the regular cast, Desi Arnaz once commented, *"I Love Lucy* was designed for her, built for her. All the rest of us are just props—Bill, Vivian, and me. Darn good props, but props."[2]

However, the series benefited from other aspects of Ball's creativity besides her comedic acting. Her instincts for shaping, writing, and directing entire shows and ongoing plotlines, as well as her business instincts, helped from the beginning to set the production's direction. She also knew how to handle such technical aspects of the show as cameras, lighting, and directing—and she was never shy about making her opinions known, even when it involved Richard Burton, Elizabeth Taylor, John Wayne, or other potentially intimidating guest stars. Ball loved to involve herself in almost every aspect of *I Love Lucy*; Bob Schiller, a longtime writer for the series, once remarked, "Lucy was the mother hen around the studio."[3]

Arnaz was nominally her equal partner, and he was responsible for many of the shrewd business moves that ensured the show's success. Furthermore, Ball was always quick to acknowledge the role her husband played in her success, as well as the parts played by the show's writers and other colleagues.

Nonetheless, everyone connected with the show understood exactly who the boss was, and they recognized the show's most important asset. Once, on the set, Ball tripped on a floor cable and stumbled slightly. Arnaz, who was always sensitive to anything that might hurt his wife, immediately noticed. After making sure she was not hurt, he wryly remarked to nearby colleagues, "Jeez, amigos, anything happens to her, and we're all in the shrimp business."[4]

INNOVATIONS

Despite Ball's dominance, the series was memorable in ways beyond simply her performances and influence. *I Love Lucy* was a pioneering show that helped change the course of television history, ushering the entertainment medium out of its infancy and into a more sophisticated era. As an editorial writer for the *New York Times* put it, Ball and her show "helped inaugurate the age of television just as surely as Charlie Chaplin helped inaugurate the age of movies."[5]

In those early days, TV consisted mostly of already established forms borrowed from other areas of entertainment. Live dramas were outgrowths of Broadway theater. Game shows and situation comedies were transplants from radio. The hosts of variety shows usually came out of vaudeville theater.

I Love Lucy helped define a new form— the situation comedy, or sitcom—and make it one of the medium's most enduring vehicles. TV sitcoms had existed before *Lucy*, but the show was so successful, and so dominated the industry, that its basic format became the model for virtually every sitcom to follow. Moreover, in the years after *Lucy*, its specific form—the thirty-minute sitcom—emerged as TV's dominant entertainment format.

The show was an influential pioneer in other ways as well. It introduced technical innovations that quickly became standard practice within the TV industry. According to author Michael McClay, "The techniques for sitcom production were created by the *I Love Lucy* staff and—except for camera technology advancement—the procedure for filming or taping television sitcoms has not essentially changed since that original team created them."[6]

MORE THAN JUST QUAINT

The premise of *I Love Lucy* was simple: Arnaz played Ricky Ricardo, a successful New York bandleader. Ball was Lucy Ricardo, his scatterbrained wife. Lucy was desperate to get out of the house and into show business, while Ricky was just as determined to keep her where she was. This

A behind-the-scenes look at I Love Lucy. *The show's technical innovations set the standard for future TV sitcoms.*

tension underscored each episode. Head writer Jess Oppenheimer recalled of an early episode, "One of the lines in the script had Desi saying, 'I want a wife who's just a wife.' That bit of dialogue pretty much summed up our basic premise."[7]

The persona that Ball created for Lucy Ricardo touched a chord in millions of viewers, appealing to a broad audience and cutting deeply across social and cultural lines. She was clumsy and unsophisticated, but she was also brave, good-hearted, lovable, and game for anything. She was always devising crazy schemes, and she had the ability to turn even the simplest task into disaster.

To sophisticated viewers today, *I Love Lucy* might seem like nothing more than a quaint, even crude relic. The plots are uncomplicated, the gags are corny, and the relationship between Lucy and Ricky Ricardo is clearly from a prefeminist, nonpolitically correct time. Viewers accustomed to modern TV's high production values, specialized cable stations, and increasingly risqué material might find *Lucy* overly simple or far too innocent.

In the 1950s, however, it was often daring, even revolutionary. Underneath its lighthearted comedy and simple premise, the show regularly explored serious themes: the tensions of married life, the

Ball (right) and costar Vivian Vance shove chocolates into their mouths and clothing in a still from the famous episode "Job Switching."

THE REDHEADED EVERYWOMAN

In his memorial piece "A Zany Redheaded Everywoman: Lucille Ball: 1911–1989," writer William A. Henry III reflects on Ball's immortal TV persona:

"She never lost touch with the insecure, self-conscious adolescent inside her and seemed most at ease when playing a zany or a frump. Her great creation was the Lucy character, a Little Scamp who was forever conniving, forever failing, forever meriting punishment yet winning forgiveness. The thwarted schemer was a figure dating back to the Romans if not the Greeks, but Ball deftly sentimentalized the character, merged its cunning intellect with joyously low physical comedy and, perhaps most important, feminized it.

Her shows—*I Love Lucy, The Lucille Ball and Desi Arnaz Show, The Lucy Show* and *Here's Lucy*—reflected the major post–World War II social trends, from the baby boom to the exodus to the suburbs to the democratization of travel. Their foremost concern was the yearning of one redheaded Everywoman to get out of the kitchen and into a job and then, once employed, to emerge from beneath the boss's thumb.

She endured any indignity in search of her big chance. The greatest indignity of all, it generally turned out, was the chuckling condescension of her husband Ricky, played by her real-life husband and business partner Desi Arnaz. The confident king of the castle, he was always ready to teach Lucy a lesson."

clash between career and home, the importance of loyalty and friendship. It also reflected important social trends of the 1950s, such as the baby boom, America's increasing obsession with celebrity, and the trend toward moving to the suburbs.

Most of all, however, the show touched a chord in viewers because it was about the love between two people. In her memoirs, Ball pointed out this fundamental element: "You have to learn to live with recognition and fame, and more important, you have to realize why you're famous. The *I Love Lucy* show was [popular because it was] love personified. It was little domestic spats and upsets happily concluded, an exaggeration of American life that came out all right."[8]

On TV, Ball and Desi Arnaz portrayed a couple who weathered marital difficulties with love and humor, but their real-life relationship was more turbulent and eventually ended in divorce.

A ROCKY PERSONAL LIFE

Her runaway hit show made Ball rich and gave her phenomenal professional success. Desilu Productions, the company she and Arnaz had formed, grew explosively in the wake of their popular sitcom. Within a few years, Desilu was in the top ranks of Hollywood studios—the largest TV production company in the world, re-sponsible for hundreds of hours of hit programs. When Ball took over Desilu in 1962, she became the first female head of a major Hollywood studio.

The comedian's personal life, unfortunately, did not always soar as high as her professional life. Ball had grown up in a loving but somewhat precarious house-hold, and all her life she desperately wanted a close family. However, her marriage to Arnaz was always rocky. They loved each other passionately but fought just as powerfully. After many years of enduring the storms, America's favorite couple finally admitted defeat and underwent a painful, very public divorce. The two remained friendly until Arnaz's death, but nonetheless Ball endured years of heartache and sadness.

She also withstood serious problems with her children, Lucie and Desi Jr. The comedian was never a natural at mothering and had difficulty maintaining close relationships with her children. As a teenager, her son became involved in scandalous encounters with drugs and older women. Her daughter, alienated by Ball's inability to connect, moved away from the house as soon as possible. Even though both children reconciled partially with her in later years, and despite a successful second marriage, Ball was never able to sustain the family she had dreamed of.

A TROUPER

Ball's personality rarely let her relax. When she sold Desilu in 1967, Ball became even wealthier than before, but she never retired. Although in her later years she spent much of her time indulging in her passion for games such as backgammon, she continued to make movies and television shows—and she never faded from the public eye.

When Ball died in 1989, at age seventy-seven, newspaper headlines around the world needed to say nothing more than LUCY DIES. Everyone knew who Lucy was, and everyone loved her—at least, they loved her television persona. In a memorial piece, Charles Champlin, the arts editor for the *Los Angeles Times*, summed up the world's opinion: "The cameras have X-ray properties, and the millions who saw and loved her were not wrong to think they perceived a generous and loving woman, as well as a glorious clown who knew the world was better off laughing."[9]

This "glorious clown" was world famous for the latter half of her life and continues to be famous long after her death. For a good portion of her life, however, Ball was simply another struggling actress, and prior to that she had a difficult and often unhappy childhood. Her story begins in Jamestown, New York, in 1911.

1 The Young Lucy

"My mother's early life, laced with tragedy and poverty, paved the way for her ambitious career goals in later years, and for her relentlessly hard work in pursuit of them."

—Lucie Arnaz

Surrounded by rolling farmland, Jamestown lies on the shore of Lake Chautauqua in southwest New York. When Lucille Ball was a child there in the early part of the twentieth century, it was a small but active manufacturing center with smoky factories turning out such products as textiles, cabinetry, and metal furniture. Jamestown was also a focal point for the many resort destinations around the lake and in the nearby Allegheny Mountains.

One of the town's more prominent residents in the late nineteenth century was Jasper Ball, Lucille Ball's paternal grandfather. Ball was a well-to-do landowner who increased his wealth by investing in phone companies in the early days of that industry. When Ball bought a telephone company in far-off Butte, Montana, his son Henry moved there to work as an electrician and lineman.

Returning to the family home in Jamestown in 1910, Henry Ball fell in love with and married an attractive young woman named Desirée Hunt. She had changed her name from its original spelling and pronunciation, Desire, and was nicknamed DeDe. DeDe's father, Fred, was a jack-of-all-trades; her mother, Flora, was a midwife.

A SWEET-TALKER IS BORN

Henry and DeDe Ball's first child, Lucille Desirée Ball, was born on August 6, 1911, in their house at 60 Stewart Avenue. However, young Lucille did not stay in Jamestown long. She spent her first few years being shuttled around the country while Henry sought work. The family lived for periods in Montana and Michigan, although their home base remained Jamestown.

Lucille was a lively child, talkative and animated even at an early age. She also had a tendency to wander away and get in trouble. To let her daughter play outside but stay close by, DeDe Ball created a system meant to serve as a sort of early warning alert. She attached Lucille to a rope and a metal runner on a wire clothesline that ran beside the house. As long as Lucille's

Lucille Ball at six months old. Ball was born in Jamestown, New York on August 6, 1911.

THE DEATH OF HER FATHER

When Lucille was still very young, her father became seriously ill with typhoid fever, an infectious disease. The family returned to Jamestown from Michigan, where they had been living, so that DeDe Ball could better care for him. But in those days before the invention of antibiotics, contracting typhoid was often a death sentence. Henry Ball passed away in February 1915.

Ball later recalled that she could barely remember her father. His death, she said, resulted in one of her earliest memories: "Doctors with black leather satchels hovered around us like moths."[12] She also had a vivid memory of a bird that flew in the window of the room on the day he died. All her adult life, Ball had a phobia about wallpaper, paintings, and anything else that depicted birds. She did not mind real birds, for some reason – only pictures of them. If given a hotel room with bird paintings, for instance, she would insist that they be removed.

In the wake of her husband's death, DeDe Ball found herself in a difficult and lonely situation. She was a widowed single mother—and she was pregnant as well. Furthermore, her husband's family, the Balls, were not eager to help her. Mother and daughter left the house on Stewart Avenue and moved back in with DeDe Ball's parents, Fred and Flora. Just before Lucille's fourth birthday, DeDe Ball gave birth to a son, whom she named Fred.

LIFE WITH GRANDMA PETERSON

Three years later DeDe Ball married again, to a factory worker named Ed Peterson.

mother (who was inside the house) could hear the metal sliding on the clothesline, she knew her child was safe.

However, the girl quickly began trying to convince passersby to let her go. "Mister, help me," she would say. "I got caught up in this silly clothesline. Can you help me out?"[10] Ball would later put this knack for sweet-talking her way out of a situation to good use on television, and apparently it worked even when she was small. Years later Ball reminisced, "I must have been pretty convincing, because I was set free a lot."[11]

A photo from 1913 shows two-year-old Ball. The comedian's spirited, talkative nature was evident even as a small child.

Peterson did not like children and refused to let them call him "Daddy." Furthermore, when he took Lucille's mother to Detroit, Michigan, where he had been promised a job, he insisted that the children remain in Jamestown. Fred was left with the Hunts, while Lucille stayed with Ed Peterson's parents.

Lucille's new stepgrandfather was such a shadowy presence in the house that he was almost nonexistent. However, Sophia Peterson, her stepgrandmother, was anything but shadowy. Tall, thin, and unsmiling, Grandma Peterson was a sternly religious, humorless woman who was of the opinion that anything pleasurable was evil. She mocked Lucille, making fun of her gangly posture and high voice. She also worked the girl hard, forcing her to complete a long list of difficult chores every day.

Lucille's intense loneliness during this period may have contributed to her life-long distaste for being alone—but it also may have contributed to her passion for theatrics. She was so lonely at the Petersons' that she invented an imaginary friend named Sassafrassa. With Sassafrassa as company, Lucille would use her precious free time for a favorite activity: inventing plays and performing all the parts.

The Petersons were not rich, and Sophia Peterson was not about to give Lucille spending money. Cash was so scarce that Lucille did not even have her own pencil at school. The shame and unhappiness this brought was so strong that decades later, when Lucille Ball was the owner of a major Hollywood studio, she still compulsively hoarded pencils—taking them from the studio she ran and keeping them in her closets at home.

FULL HOUSE

In 1922 DeDe and Ed Peterson returned to Jamestown and rescued Lucille from this dispiriting life. DeDe Peterson had come back to care for her ailing mother, Flora

Hunt; unfortunately, Flora died soon after their return. Their mother and stepfather took Lucille and Fred back, and the newly reunited family moved into a small house on Eighth Street in the nearby village of Celoron. (This street is now called Lucy Lane.)

The Celoron home was a comfortable place and a much happier environment for Lucille. The household was lively and colorful despite the loss of Flora, whom Lucille and her mother had dearly loved, and even with the withdrawn presence of Lucille's stepfather, Ed Peterson, who spent most of his free time drinking quietly.

Part of the reason for this liveliness was that Lucille's mother, a vivacious music lover, remained energetic and cheerful throughout it all. She worked in one of Jamestown's classiest dress shops and so was always in style despite the family's relative lack of money. Furthermore, other family members shared the house. DeDe's sister Lola Hunt operated a beauty parlor in the home, and the house was rounded out by Lola's daughter, Cleo Hunt, who was close in age to Lucille and Fred, and the family patriarch, grandfather Fred Hunt.

Lucille adored her grandfather. He became a surrogate father figure to her to such a degree that she called him "Daddy." Daddy Hunt was a lively character who held a variety of jobs over the years, including mailman, hotel manager, factory woodworker, and grocery-store operator. He was also a confirmed socialist and a pro-union organizer. Cleo Hunt recalled him as "an enormously earthy,

THE FAKE BANDAGE

Biographer Kathleen Brady, in this excerpt from her book Lucille: The Life of Lucille Ball, *relates a performance by a teenaged Ball of an apparent domestic disaster. The incident took place at a friend's house in Jamestown, where a party was under way. Ed was her stepfather, Ed Peterson, and a "Hoosier cabinet" was a kind of kitchen cupboard:*

"She arrived late and in tears. . . . When she finally arrived at the party, she was holding a bandaged hand and whimpering. 'You know how Ed puts his razor on top of the Hoosier cabinet instead of taking it up to the bathroom?' she asked her sympathetic friends. 'Well, just what my mother said would happen finally did. After I washed the dishes I shut the door, and the razor came down and cut my face and hand.'

They fussed over her, patted her shoulder, and brought her lemonade. When Lucille began picking at the bandage, Pauline protested, but Lucille kept playing with it and finally ripped it away, revealing no cut. She had made the whole thing up and delivered her first believable performance of a household misadventure."

humorous man with a great sense of roots and heritage."[13]

FIRST PERFORMANCES AND EARLY INFLUENCES

The children in the house were very close and remained so all their lives. After she became famous, Ball employed both her brother and her cousin in various capacities. She called Cleo her sister all her life.

Since all the adults worked, the children were often left on their own, a situation that scandalized the neighbors. They were also responsible for many of the household chores. As the oldest, Lucille shouldered the most responsibility, a trait that would continue into adulthood. She later recalled, "I suddenly found myself in her [Grandmother Hunt's] shoes, at the age of eleven. . . . So it was my job to make the beds, do the dusting, make sure the table was set, cook dinner, and do the supper dishes."[14]

There was, however, time for play. A bright but erratic student, Lucille did not like to study, and no one in the house forced her to. She was always more interested in work, and threw herself into it with vigor. As an adolescent she held a variety of part-time jobs, including selling hot dogs and hamburgers at a concession stand in the local park.

Though the family had seen its share of loss and financial struggle, DeDe Peterson (left, shown here with Ball) kept an upbeat attitude.

In Kathleen Brady's Lucille: The Life of Lucille Ball, *Ball's brother, Fred, reminisces about his childhood days. The encouragement of independence, standing up for oneself, and forthright speech that the Ball children learned early on would become a hallmark of Lucille Ball's adult behavior.*

"We were taught from the beginning to take care of ourselves. That was probably the attribute that caused Lucille to be successful. The most important thing I learned from the family was to put problems on the table, right up front. The idea was: Don't harbor. If you've got a comment, complaint, criticism, put it on the table. I can't remember when we ever had an extensive argument. Discussions, yes, but no catastrophic differences of opinion."

Lucille was even more enthusiastic about appearing in shows. One of her first public roles was when she played an angel in a school performance. She and her siblings and friends also loved to make their own shows, staging plays on the staircase of their house or creating a circus in the backyard by the chicken coop. Later, as a student at Jamestown High School, she formed a drama club and wrote a play, casting herself in the lead as well as directing it.

As a performer, Lucille was deeply influenced by the circuses, vaudeville variety shows, and silent films that passed through Jamestown and the Celoron Amusement Park near her house. She later recalled how thrilled she was by these first tastes of real show business: "Wow! I knew I had to be part of it."[15] She was especially taken by a well-known comedian of the day, Julius Tannen. Tannen was famous for his deadpan delivery of monologues and stories. She later said of his impact on her, when she saw him perform in Jamestown: "Tannen was magic. . . . He changed my life. I knew it was a very serious, wonderful thing to be able to make people laugh and cry, to be able to play on their emotions."[16]

DRAMA SCHOOL

As a teenager Lucille was often bold, adventurous, and rebellious. She was the first in her class to get a bobbed hairstyle, which in the so-called Roaring Twenties was a daring sign of independence and stylishness. At fourteen she started going out with a twenty-one-year-old named Johnny DeVita. DeVita had a wild reputation—he ran bootleg whiskey from Canada (at the time, Prohibition banned alcohol in America), and he may have had minor ties to organized crime. Lucille's connection with him scandalized even her relatively easygoing family.

Meanwhile, Lucille's love of theatrics had blossomed into dreams of becoming a Broadway actress. In the autumn of 1926, at the age of fifteen, she temporarily dropped out of Jamestown High School and left for New York City. She had $50 sewn into her underwear. Her family encouraged the move, perhaps to get her away from the influence of Johnny DeVita. In any event, cousin Cleo recalled, "Nothing would have stopped her. If DeDe hadn't sent her, she would have run away."[17]

Lucille enrolled in the John Murray Anderson–Robert Milton Drama School. Milton, a theater director, and Anderson, a theater producer, were well-regarded pros. At their academy aspiring actresses studied subjects such as diction, voice, dramatic interpretation, fencing, and makeup. One of the school's star pupils was eighteen-year-old Bette Davis, soon to become world famous.

Ball did not thrive there, however. She was shy and fearful, intimidated by older and more experienced students like Davis. Strangely, considering her general enthusiasm for hard work, she also disliked the discipline required by the tough classes. Among the exercises Lucille was forced to do were vocal drills designed to dispense with her western New York accent, which turned "water" into "worter" and "horses" into "hasses."

Ball was such an unpromising student, in fact, that soon after her arrival, Anderson wrote to DeDe Peterson, gently informing her that her daughter had no talent and advising that she go home. After

A young Bette Davis (pictured) was one of Ball's classmates at the John Murray Anderson–Robert Milton Drama School in New York.

only a month, Lucille did just that, resuming her studies at Jamestown High School. "All I learned in drama school," she later recalled, "was how to be frightened."[18]

NEW YORK AGAIN

In the summer of 1927, while Ball was still in high school, a tragedy tore her family's household apart. While Fred and a few other young people were by the side of the house, looking at a .22 rifle that Fred had recently received for his birthday, a boy was accidentally shot and paralyzed. Grandfather Hunt was held responsible, since he was the only adult present at the time. Sentenced to pay the boy's medical expenses, he lost the house in Celoron and was forced to declare bankruptcy.

Lucille, her mother, her brother, and Ed Peterson moved out and found a cramped apartment in Jamestown. The happy, full house that Ball had savored after her unpleasant period with Grandma Peterson would never be restored. About the tragic incident, Ball later recalled, "It ruined Celoron for us; it destroyed our life together there."[19]

Despite her ignoble performance at drama school, Ball was still determined to try her hand again in the New York theater world. She returned there as often as finances allowed, looking for a break. She also adopted a new, more glamorous identity for herself: she took the stage name Diane Belmont (in honor of a famous racetrack near New York City) and claimed that Butte, Montana, was her hometown.

"SPARKLING ACTION AND LINES"

Two reviews of one of Ball's early public performances, in an amateur theater version of the play Within the Law *in June 1930, indicate the vivid acting for which she would become known. Reprinted in Kathleen Brady's* Lucille: The Life of Lucille Ball, *they are probably the first appearances in print of a review of the future star:*

"From the *Jamestown Morning Post*: 'Miss Lucille Ball, as Agnes Lynch, a particularly hardboiled little crook, who is undergoing a process of refinement . . . was also admirable. Miss Ball's acting furnished the comedy relief so necessary in the play of the intensity of *Within the Law*.'

From the *Chautauqua Daily*: 'Miss Ball gave one of the most impressive portrayals of the evening; she lived the part of the underworld girl with as much realism as if it were her regular existence. It was her sparkling action and lines that brought continued applause from her audience at her first exit of the (second) act and again in the last act. . . .

The high spot of *Within the Law* was undoubtedly the start of the last scene with the interview of Agnes Lynch and Inspector Burke. Lucille Ball played with even more enthusiasm than before and put her part across to the audience in the best manner of the evening. In a role that required action, and a good deal of it, she exhibited remarkable maturity and poise.'"

Times were tough for an unknown girl in the big city, however, especially now that America was gripped in the economic woes of the Great Depression. Ball lived in a succession of cheap boardinghouses, hoarding her pennies and taking occasional jobs such as jerking sodas in drugstores to tide her over between acting jobs.

Sometimes things were so rough that she had to sneak food. Ball developed a trick of hanging out at lunch counters where two doughnuts came free with a nickel cup of coffee. She would wait until a patron who had left a doughnut uneaten was leaving, then casually slide onto his stool and eat the doughnut while requesting a refill on the coffee. She paid for the new cup of coffee with the former patron's tip, receiving two more doughnuts.

When she did find work as an actress, it was only in tiny nonspeaking parts. Ball was slender and pretty, so she sometimes got occasional work as one of a line of chorus girls with musical revues such as Earl Carroll's *Vanities* and the *Ziegfeld Follies*. But to succeed, chorus girls needed to be sparkly and vivacious. Ball was too frightened and bashful, so no speaking roles came her way. As she put it later, "Years ago before I came to Hollywood I was a showgirl. But just before a new revue of musical would start, I'd always get fired. I was shy and had no personality— I don't blame them."[20]

BECOMING A FLAPPER

Lonely and unable to catch a break, Ball returned to Jamestown in time to reenroll as a high school sophomore. However, she dropped out before she could graduate. Instead, she worked part-time at various odd jobs around Jamestown, such as running a department-store elevator and selling cosmetics. She also rekindled her romance with Johnny DeVita.

Ball moved into her own apartment when she was nineteen. She had become, in many ways, a typical '30s-era "flapper"—a young woman who indulged in such scandalous behavior as bobbing her hair, abandoning corsets, and drinking and smoking in public. Such women were called "flappers" because they wore big boots with flapping, unfastened buckles.

Despite her disappointments in New York City, Ball did not abandon the theater. She landed parts in several amateur productions in Jamestown and at the nearby Chautauqua Institution, a summer institute of the arts and philosophy that had originally been a camp for Methodist ministers.

She received favorable notices in these shows, although she was somewhat hampered by a mysterious disease that flared up during this period. It may have been rheumatic fever or rheumatoid arthritis; a firm diagnosis was never made, and Ball told several different versions of the story of her illness over the years. Whatever it was, the illness made it difficult for her to walk, and it forced her to wear heavy orthopedic shoes for a time to build up her leg muscles.

Ball also returned to New York City periodically. She never had luck with her theatrical ambitions, but eventually she did land steady work as a model for coats and dresses. Even during the Great Depression, New York's garment industry thrived, and work for clothing models was plentiful. Ball's slender figure and striking looks proved to be a valuable aid when auditioning for these jobs.

STILL SNEAKING FOOD

Ball's most reliable work was with one of the city's best-known clothing designers, Hattie Carnegie. Carnegie liked Ball because she bore a strong resemblance to a popular film star, Constance Bennett. Bennett was a regular customer of Carnegie's and often stopped at the dressmaker's shop to inspect the latest designs. Ball's tall and elegantly lean figure showed off these dresses beautifully, and Carnegie encouraged Ball to become the regular model whenever Bennett was in town for a shopping spree. Ball even dyed her hair blond from its natural chestnut to further her resemblance to the movie star.

In addition to this job, Ball also had some success as a photographic model. A special honor was being chosen as one of the models for a prestigious nationwide ad campaign, the Chesterfield Cigarette Girls. Between the work for Hattie Carnegie and her other modeling jobs, Ball was beginning to bring in regular money.

However, the aspiring model and actress still had to scrimp. She lived in a tiny apartment that she shared with a friend from Jamestown. She ate sparingly—in part because she needed to stay thin for her work, but also simply because she had so little cash. Furthermore, she still had to sneak food. For instance, she depended on dinner dates to buy her decent meals.

Ball's tall, slender figure helped her land steady work modeling clothes for designer Hattie Carnegie (pictured).

(She later re-created and made fun of this experience in the movie *Stage Door*.) From other models, she learned to use these dates as occasions to stock up on supplies for the week. She would hide a napkin in her purse or line it with wax paper, then sneak rolls, meat, and other food into it when no one was looking.

THE BREAK

Despite the precariousness of Ball's existence as a New York model, there were bright spots. For one thing, her brother

Ball as a model. Though modeling provided a regular income, money was still tight and Ball sometimes had to sneak extra food home from restaurants.

and mother, with whom she remained close, came to stay with her for extended periods. This helped soothe the loneliness she still felt by being separated from familiar surroundings.

Also, Ball's time in New York gave her the opportunity to become friends with a number of glamorous, nonconformist characters who made the city their home. They exposed her to a variety of new ex-periences and opened up new possibilities. Some of these characters also became sweethearts, and Ball had a long series of romances. She nearly eloped with one boyfriend—a dashing British photographer named Roger Furse. The comedian once remarked of this period in her life, "I was *always* falling in love."[21]

Ball's first big break in the theater came from three thousand miles away. In the summer of 1933, she ran into an acquaintance, an agent named Sylvia Hahlo. Ball had just been chosen as a Chesterfield Girl, and on the strength of this distinction, Hahlo recommended that she answer an upcoming theatrical casting call. Chorus girls were needed to appear as slave women in ancient Rome for an upcoming film, *Roman Scandals*. The movie was set to be shot in Hollywood later that

Ball's first movie role was as a slave in the film Roman Scandals, *starring Eddie Cantor (pictured).*

summer. Its star was an enormously popular entertainer, the saucer-eyed comedian and singer Eddie Cantor.

By the time Ball applied for the job, the dozen chorus girls that were needed had already been chosen and were set to leave for the West Coast shortly. One dropped out at the last moment, however, and Ball was selected to take her place. The choice was made without extensive testing beforehand. "Fortunately," Ball joked in her memoirs, "there was no time for a screen test, or I might never have been accepted."[22]

CALIFORNIA BOUND

The job was only for a short period of time; six weeks had been scheduled for the movie's shooting. However, the pay was excellent. Ball would be getting three times the $100 average weekly salary she was accustomed to. This was a lavish amount of money for the depression years. Besides the boost in wages, the prospect of a jaunt by train to California, escaping the heat and humidity of New York, was appealing. Ball thought of the trip as a lark, little more than a paid vacation.

She boarded her train for the cross-country trip with the other chorus girls in cheerful anticipation, but without any idea of the long-term consequences. The trip, she assumed, would be a short, pleasant holiday, and she expected to return to New York in time for the fall fashion season. Instead, the journey marked the true beginning of her professional career—and the next time she returned east would be as a rising movie starlet.

2 "Queen of the B's"

"Say yes to everything. Do everything you're asked to do without complaining. Learn something new about your trade every day. Study hard, and work harder."

—Lucille Ball's secrets of success

Ball immediately liked the atmosphere she found on arrival in Hollywood. For one thing, Los Angeles was still a small town in the 1930s, an informal place of low buildings and orange groves. Its informality and friendliness reminded her of the small-town character of Jamestown, homey attributes that she had missed in New York City.

The weather also agreed with her. Instead of the muggy summers and bitter winters of New York, Los Angeles had bright sunshine, balmy temperatures, the blue Pacific Ocean, and clean air. "Nobody thought of smog in those days," Ball later recalled. "Like TV, it didn't exist."[23]

Best of all, Hollywood was the center of the glamorous movie industry. The town's great studios, such as MGM and RKO, each churned out dozens of films a year. This parade of comedies, dramas, and musicals softened the edges of the depression's harshness for millions of people around the world.

Among those employed by the movie industry were scores of young and hopeful actors just like Ball, and she readily found kindred spirits. For a stagestruck young woman such as herself, Hollywood must have seemed perfect.

MAKING THE FIRST MOVIE

When Ball reported to the MGM lot to fulfill her role in *Roman Scandals*, she soon discovered that she enjoyed the work. Not only that—she was also good at it. Even with her head partially obscured in a long, flowing blond wig (as were those of the other slave girls), Ball proved to be naturally at ease in front of the movie camera.

She was such a natural, in fact, that she was chosen out of the pack to take part in a bit of physical comedy that Cantor, the star, dreamed up. In it, she was hit in the face with a flying gob of mud. (This segment was cut from the final film, although Ball can be briefly seen with mud on her face.) She was also the only slave girl who was given any dialogue—only two lines, but lines nonetheless. Ball's screen debut thus included the immortal words "He

"Stick-to-Itness"

In this passage from Kathleen Brady's Lucille: The Life of Lucille Ball, *the comedian comments on how her willingness to try anything for the camera earned her recognition early in her career, during the filming of her first movies:*

"My stick-to-itness came out here. Suddenly I was in show business. It interested me because I was learning, and . . . I never complained. Whatever they asked me, I did. I did one line, two lines, with animals, in mud packs, seltzer in the face. Eddie Cantor noticed it first at Goldwyn. He'd say 'Give it to that girl, she doesn't mind.' I took it all as a learning time."

says the city put us here and we should live here" and "Eddie's coming! Eddie's coming!"[24]

The shooting time for *Roman Scandals* went long past its allotted schedule. The original six weeks stretched into several months. This was mainly because the movie's choreographer, the brilliant but eccentric Busby Berkeley, was stretched thin with multiple projects; he was also distracted by frequent drinking bouts.

The delay in the project suited Ball fine. It gave her time to begin learning how things operated within the small, tightly knit world of movie making. She quickly realized that her chances of being a success would improve tremendously if she could figure out how to be noticed as someone special. She was not the most glamorous or curvaceous of the twelve slave girls, but she thought of other ways to stand out.

For instance, Ball learned that the studio's chief, the legendary Sam Goldwyn, was coming to inspect her group one day.

On the set of Roman Scandals, *Ball used her humor to make herself stand out to Sam Goldwyn (pictured), head of MGM Studios.*

Rather than simply trying to impress him with her beauty, she sought to turn what she saw as a liability into a comic asset, by making fun of her relatively flat chest. She stuffed the top of her swimsuit with toilet paper, gloves, and socks before lining up with the others, then made sure some of the wadding was peeking out when Goldwyn came by. Ball wryly recalled, "He noticed me."[25]

HAVING A WONDERFUL TIME

The aspiring actress was happy for the delay in the schedule in other ways as well. For one thing, she was making excellent money—and putting it aside. Many of the other chorus girls were spending their salaries right away on luxuries such as furs and cars, but Ball maintained her frugal ways. Instead of buying a car, for instance, she got around on a bicycle or by hitchhiking. She was also delighted when she found lodging in a house near the studio where she could have kitchen privileges. It meant that she could save more by not eating in restaurants all the time.

Despite this frugality, however, Ball loved to go out at night with others from the set. This was another reason she was hoping *Roman Scandals* would continue to be delayed—she was making friends and enjoying herself thoroughly. When out with friends and coworkers, Ball's shyness seemed to vanish. She turned into a raconteur—a masterful, amusing storyteller. She found that she had a knack for holding an audience spellbound by telling lengthy, convoluted tales. These stories, typically told to friends over dinner, marked a blossoming of Ball's zestful comedy style.

Typically, Ball would dramatically recount the events of her day and poke good-natured fun at herself. An important part of this storytelling, biographer Kathleen Brady notes, was a sense of wild exaggeration: "She was never just hungry, she was so famished that she could chew on the wall. She was never just surprised, she was so shocked that she would not have batted an eye if President Roosevelt waited on their table."[26]

CONTRACT PLAYER

By the time *Roman Scandals* finished shooting, Ball was thoroughly smitten with the Hollywood way of life, and she decided she wanted to stay in Los Angeles. She was sufficiently bolstered by her success in making her first movie to expect steady work as an actress. She missed her family, but she was making so much money that she felt confident about saving up enough to bring them out to Los Angeles.

Her expectations about steady work were met. MGM, which had produced *Roman Scandals*, signed Ball up as a contract player. Under the studio system then in practice in Hollywood, contract workers were given a modest weekly wage in exchange for brief appearances in movies, most of them utterly forgettable. Only a few actors out of this large pool of hopefuls ever got noticed and advanced to the rank of top-flight star.

Ball's resemblance to movie star Constance Bennett helped her acting career just as it had her modeling. Ball (left) worked as a double for Bennett (right).

Some of the movies that Ball appeared in were shorts, called "two-reelers," while others were feature-length films. Some were silly romantic comedies (with titles like *Hold that Girl*), others were grim crime dramas (*Blood Money*) or costumed "period" stories (*Affairs of Cellini*). Occasionally she was "loaned" to other studios—that is, allowed to appear in movies produced outside of MGM. More than once she worked as a double for Constance Bennett, the star who had once bought the dresses that Ball had modeled in New York.

The young actress was kept busy, and she worked hard. Shooting movies is notoriously dull work for unknown rank-and-file workers. It involves long hours of waiting around, being fitted into costumes and made up, then waiting more before shooting brief scenes. Often the same shots had to be filmed over and over again. Never afraid of hard work, Ball shouldered the workload and kept any complaints to herself.

Settling in L.A.

As she worked on diverse movies in a variety of settings, Ball began to slowly develop a distinctive style. Much of this came from watching other actresses and studying their styles. One particular influence was the great comedian Carole Lombard, who became a close friend of Ball's.

Lombard's blend of sophistication and sauciness made her one of Hollywood's most successful stars in the 1930s and early '40s. She was a profound model for Ball's still-emerging style long before they met.

After they became friends, Lombard influenced the slightly younger Ball in other ways as well. She would often advise Ball on matters ranging from studio etiquette to dealing with boyfriends to dressing stylishly but economically. She also helped Ball secure a number of plum roles. Lombard continued to be one of Ball's best friends and strongest mentors until her death in a plane crash in 1942.

As she learned from more experienced actresses like Lombard, Ball gradually became accustomed to the business ways of Hollywood. Her personal life also became more settled. She rented a small house on Ogden Drive, north of Sunset Boulevard. She acquired a fox terrier named Toy. She also had a string of romances, including affairs with two young actors, Broderick Crawford and William Holden, and two older men who were longtime Hollywood insiders: producer Pandro S. Berman and director Alexander Hall.

Ball's brother, Fred, came out to live with her, and eventually Ball brought her mother out as well. (DeDe had separated from Ed Peterson and was working in a department store in Washington, D.C.) Ball had hoped to be rich by the time she brought her mother out, but she was not

Carole Lombard, one of Ball's greatest influences and best friends. Ball developed her own style by observing Lombard's work.

quite there yet. The actress did pick DeDe up from the train station in a limousine and treat her to a lavish welcoming dinner. In order to do it, however, she had to borrow both the limousine and the money from a friend, actor George Raft.

Soon after, Ball's cousin Cleo and her grandfather, "Daddy" Fred Hunt, joined the little family. After years of separation, Ball finally had her family in one place again. From this point on, she assumed responsibility for keeping her family together, financially and otherwise, and she insisted on maintaining constant closeness. "It was important for her to have us all together," Cleo recalled, "and wherever she went, it was 'Mama, come with me.' Lucy needed that."[27]

Moving to Columbia

By now, about a year after arriving in Hollywood, Ball could consider herself a professional—a steadily working actress. She was far from being a star, however. She had not yet even gotten her name listed in the credits at the end of a movie. Furthermore, Ball was bored with the minor, often passive roles MGM cast her in. She was not happy being just another pretty face and body, interchangeable with any of dozens of others. "I was tired of being a bewigged and bejeweled mannequin," she recalled later. "I wanted *action*."[28]

When her contract with the studio expired in 1934, Ball signed on with another studio, Columbia. At Columbia she was still just a contract player, and she earned only $75 a week—less than she had been getting at MGM. However, she saw a contract with Columbia as a better chance for career advancement. True, the studio had a reputation for churning out low-budget and often low-quality pictures; on the other hand, it allowed its contract players greater freedom in matters such as choosing roles, unlike MGM.

Her career with Columbia included small roles in several comedies, including *Three Little Pigskins* with the Three Stooges. (She claimed that the only thing her experience with this manic comic trio taught her was that seltzer water squirted up the nose hurts a lot.) She also had a tiny role in one genuine classic, director Frank Capra's horse-racing comedy-drama *Broadway Bill*. Sharp-eyed viewers can spot the still-blond Ball as a telephone operator.

First Screen Credit

Ball's tenure at Columbia, however, was relatively brief. The studio suddenly and inexplicably dropped her along with about fifteen other contract players. She scrambled to find work and found it at another studio, RKO, which had a reputation for turning out some of the highest-quality pictures in town. Her first role there was as a model in a 1935 musical, *Roberta*. This movie is a memorable classic, starring Irene Dunne and the then-new dancing team of Ginger Rogers and Fred Astaire.

Ball worked steadily at RKO, but she was never able to hit her stride there. She was striking, but she was not classically beautiful enough to be a star—at least not according to the standards of the era. Furthermore, producers and directors still thought of her strictly as an actress. Her gift for comedy had not yet been realized. She recalled that she was usually typecast because of her looks and voice: "I started as a model because I looked like a model, and 'the other woman' or 'the career girl' because I have a deep aggressive voice that has no softness or romance in it."[29]

As a result of such typecasting, Ball worked regularly, but she did not warrant leading roles or extended close-up shots. She did not even get a screen billing until 1935's *Carnival*, where she is credited as "The Nurse."

There were many other small roles for Ball during this period, including parts in two more Rogers-Astaire movies. For these she played one of the eager young women dancing with military men (in *Follow the Fleet*) and a florist's assistant (in *Top Hat*).

MOVING UP

Even though Ball was still far from earning star billing, she was moving slowly but steadily up. In the meantime, RKO Studios kept her busy with the obligations of a rising starlet. Her shooting schedules—there were usually several at a given time—kept her busy from early in the morning well into the night. When not on the set, the studio kept her occupied with other chores, such as posing for publicity photos, meeting with directors and

Ball (second row, second from right) in Roberta, *a 1935 musical starring Ginger Rogers, Fred Astaire, and Irene Dunne.*

THREE MODELS

In Lucille: The Life of Lucille Ball, *biographer Kathleen Brady comments in the passage on how Ball began to absorb lessons in acting from three great movie actresses, Irene Dunne, Katharine Hepburn, and Carole Lombard:*

"Watching from the sidelines, Lucille saw Dunne do take after take, the same scene fifteen or twenty times, and each runthrough surprised her, because Dunne acted each different from the time before. Studying Dunne's technique led Lucille to begin to think about the different ways of reading and delivering lines.

Lucille had also managed to get on the set of a Hepburn movie, and saw that this star telegraphed whenever she was about to be funny and played a scene the same way over and over, no matter how often it was done. Earlier, Lombard impressed Lucille by managing to believe with consummate faith everything she said or did before the cameras so that she seemed ever fresh in her line reading. Lucille decided she would do best to follow Lombard's technique, yet Dunne's resourcefulness continued to amaze her."

Ball studied and admired the acting technique of movie star Irene Dunne (pictured).

producers about upcoming projects, and taking lessons (provided by the studio) on poise or methods for properly conducting interviews.

In her spare time, Ball made further changes in her personal life. She had her badly crooked teeth fixed and straightened, a year-long process that included having nine porcelain caps fitted. She also found her own apartment. Meanwhile, her brother and cousin also found separate lodgings. Ball kept the rental house on Ogden Drive, however, so that her mother and grandfather had a place of their own.

"Daddy" Fred Hunt had suffered a series of strokes, and he was increasingly fragile and ailing. However, he never lost his passionate interest in socialism and in the rights of the working class. This resulted in his habit of telling cleaning women and nurses (hired by Ball to help him) that their jobs were beneath them. Many agreed and promptly quit. As a result, Ball constantly needed to find new help for her grandfather. She recalled,"We couldn't keep a maid because he'd immediately tell her she was overworked and underpaid."[30]

BUSY B

One of Ball's best roles from this period— in many ways, her breakthrough role as a film actress—was in 1937's *Stage Door*. It gave Ball her highest billing to date, providing her with a significant role in a lively, well-written comedy-drama about aspiring actresses who room together in New York. Others in the cast included two established stars, Ginger Rogers and Katharine Hepburn, as well as two future stars, Eve Arden and Ann Miller.

Stage Door was, without much doubt, the classiest and most prestigious vehicle Ball had yet been in. The movie was a success financially as well as artistically, collecting rave reviews and popularity at the box office. At the next Academy Awards presentation, it received four Oscar nominations.

The movie also gave Ball the chance to poke fun at her early days as a would-be actress in New York. Her character, Judy Canfield, is good-hearted and down-to-earth, wise but wary. She is able to eat square meals only by accepting a steady stream of country-bumpkin dinner dates arriving in the big city from her hometown—far-off Seattle, Washington. The role was remarkably close to Ball's own experiences in New York, when she pretended to be from Montana and really did survive by stealing food while on dates.

The success of *Stage Door*, and Ball's prominent role in it, led almost immediately to bigger and better opportunities. She was still a contract player for RKO, but she was able to command much higher salaries than before—she was soon earning $1,000 to $2,000 a week, an exceptional sum in a nation not yet recovered from the depression.

Ball also began to be cast in starring, or at least featured, roles. Starting in 1938, she made a long string of movies that earned her the nickname "Queen of the B's." (The coiner of this nickname is unknown; it may have been another actor.)

Ball (left) and Ginger Rogers in Stage Door. *The film was a turning point in Ball's career, leading to bigger, better-paying roles.*

A "B movie" was (and still is) a low-budget, quickly made production, almost always with a predictable plotline and stock characters. Typically, big stars did not appear in them; roles in B movies were reserved for up-and-coming actors or has-beens who no longer garnered star billing and prime scripts.

RKO made dozens of these movies, which were sometimes also called "pro-grammers." They were popular with movie-theater owners, who liked to offer double bills to their audiences. Movies were at their peak of popularity during the depression, when for many people they, and perhaps radio, were the only form of entertainment available. However, impoverished audiences had to be coaxed to part with their money, and so double bills became increasingly popular because they

(Left to right) Ball, Harpo Marx, and Frank Albertson in Room Service, *one of the many B movies she appeared in.*

provided extra value. Theater owners had to pay more to exhibit a top-drawer, A-level picture with big stars, but they could satisfy their audiences by rounding off a double bill with a cheaper B movie.

STARRING LUCILLE BALL

The movies Ball made as a star or featured performer in the wake of *Stage Door* are, if nothing else, notable for the speed with which she made them. She performed in eleven pictures between May 1938 and December 1939—only a little more than a year and a half. Like other busy contract workers, she made so many movies, so quickly, that RKO's costume department was usually preparing two or three separate wardrobes for her simultaneously at any given moment.

Most of these movies were fairly mediocre. In the crime drama *Twelve Crowded Hours*, she plays the sister of a small-time hoodlum sent to jail by her reporter boyfriend. In the suspense adventure film *Five Came Back*, she plays a good-hearted floozy who is one of the passengers on an airplane downed in the Amazon jungle.

A few stand out more vividly because they are some of the first films to show off Ball's emerging talent for comedy. In *The Affairs of Annabel* and *Annabel Takes a Tour*, for instance, she plays a scatterbrained actress who takes part in a series of increasingly wacky publicity stunts that inevitably backfire. Another comedy, *Room Service*, created an intriguing combination by pairing Ball with three of the movie world's greatest comic subversives, the Marx Brothers. The film was not a complete success—the script was weak, muting the Marx Brothers' trademark zaniness—but Ball's second-billed role gave critics and audiences a tantalizing taste of what she could do.

Critics began to recognize her talents, and they complained when RKO continued to cast her in mediocre films. Typical was the reaction to *Beauty for the Asking*, about a beautician who invents a successful wrinkle cream. The critic for the *New York Daily News* lamented the poor script and commented, "Miss Ball rises high enough above her material to remind us that she is of the stuff that stars are made of."[31]

A Turning Point

By the end of the '30s, Ball had appeared in a total of forty-three films, few of them real classics. Her ironic nickname— "Queen of the B's"—seemed sadly true.

Thanks to years of determination and hard work, Ball had become a well-known and steadily working actress. She made good money and lived a rich life. Among her Hollywood friends were such luminaries as Ginger Rogers, Carole Lombard, George Burns and Gracie Allen, and silent-film legends Buster Keaton and Eddie Sedgwick. Nonetheless, it was beginning to look as if Ball might never achieve the first rank of stardom. At twenty-eight, she was getting rather old—by the then-current standards of Hollywood, at least—and it seemed that real fame might elude her. Then things changed dramatically, when Ball met a charming young Cuban musician named Desi Arnaz.

3 Lucy and Desi

"We would love furiously and fight furiously."

—Desi Arnaz

Desiderio Alberto Arnaz y de Acha III, as he was christened, was born in 1917 in Santiago, the second largest city in Cuba. Unusually for the time and place, he was an only child. He was raised in an atmosphere of wealth and privilege: his father was the mayor, his uncle the chief of police, his mother both a great beauty and the daughter of an executive in the powerful Bacardi rum company. Until he was a teenager, Desi led a princely life of luxury that included boats and horses, mansions and servants.

FROM CUBA TO AMERICA

This pampered life ended in 1933, when a revolution brought the dictator Fulgencio Batista to power in Cuba. Any politician connected with the old regime, Desi's father included, was stripped of possessions and rights. The Arnaz family was forced to abandon their home and possessions, and Desi's father was briefly jailed.

After the senior Arnaz was released, the family resettled in Miami, Florida. They

were poor, and Desi's father was forced to take a variety of menial jobs. While he finished high school, Desi also found odd work, including cleaning canary cages and driving a banana truck. (One of his Miami school friends was Sonny Capone, son of the notorious gangster Al Capone.)

A talented guitarist and percussionist from an early age, Desi also began singing in public. Cuban music was enjoying a vogue in America, and Arnaz capitalized on this boom. His reputation as a singer and conga drummer grew, enhanced by his personable style, athletic build, and good looks.

Arnaz's big break came when he was cast in a hit Broadway musical comedy, *Too Many Girls*. By coincidence, Ball saw this show before she met its handsome second male lead. In her memoir, Ball wrote that he "sang with a heavy Spanish accent, danced a way-out conga, banged a bongo drum, and strummed a guitar. From the way girls reacted to him, he was the Elvis Presley of his day."[32]

THE ODD COUPLE

When RKO Studios bought the rights to *Too Many Girls* in 1940, Arnaz was invited

(Left to right) Ann Miller, Desi Arnaz, and Ball in Too Many Girls. *Ball met Arnaz when she read for a role in the musical comedy.*

to appear in the film version. He jumped at the chance and brought with him to Hollywood his mother and his fiancée, a dancer named Renée de Marco.

He met Ball when she arrived to read for a part in *Too Many Girls*. She happened to be costumed for a role as a seedy burlesque performer in another film, *Dance, Girl, Dance*. The outfit included a slinky gold lamé dress and a fake black eye. Arnaz was not dazzled, but Ball's reaction was different: "I was impressed with him, though, and I must admit that I fell in love with Desi—wham, bang—in about five minutes."[33]

The next time they saw each other, Ball was in street clothes, and Arnaz's attention was riveted. According to legend, he exclaimed to a friend that she was "a hunk of woman." Never shy with the opposite sex, Arnaz walked up and asked if she knew how to rumba. He then invited her to go dancing and out to dinner. Within days Arnaz dumped his fiancée and Ball discarded her boyfriend.

They were an unlikely pair. Ball was grounded, conservative, and practical; Arnaz was reckless, bold, and daring. She relied on hard work to achieve success; he counted on lucky breaks. She was blunt and tactless, while he could charm anyone. The relationship, in many ways, ran counter to Ball's previous romances. Most of her boyfriends had been older men, often well-known producers or directors who could further her career. Now, however, she was taking up with a largely unknown musician six years younger than herself. Biographer Kathleen Brady comments, "This strange involvement, in no way calculated to help her career, was a rare instance of her not putting her work first."[34]

MORE THAN SIX MONTHS

Few of Ball's friends and colleagues expected the romance to survive. When the cast of *Too Many Girls* formed a betting pool on how long it would last, actor Eddie Bracken won because he had chosen the longest amount of time—six months.

The couple defied the odds and continued to be together as much as possible. Merging two busy schedules was difficult, however. Arnaz was frequently touring with a band he had formed, and Ball was shooting four or more pictures a year. When RKO offered Arnaz a three-picture deal, he was delighted, since it meant he could spend more time in Hollywood.

The couple's relationship was intense from the very beginning—stormy fights alternating with stormy romance. Often the fights centered around jealousy; Ball was always suspicious of Arnaz's charm with women, and he disliked the idea of her having even a casual friendship with another man. Arnaz wrote in his memoirs, "How the hell we survived this period after all this [fighting] and still had the guts to get married, I'll never understand."[35]

But marry they did, late in 1940—some six months after their first meeting. The series of crazy circumstances surrounding the wedding ceremony—comic mishaps followed by a happy ending—foreshadowed the fictional scrapes the couple would later devise for television.

A STANDING OVATION AND A NEW HOME

Arnaz wanted to marry Ball while he was performing several shows a day at a New York theater, the Roxy. The only free time he had was in the morning, though, so he and Ball rushed early one morning to Connecticut, which had no waiting period for a marriage license. However, the required blood tests took longer than expected, and then their justice of the peace decided that his office was not romantic enough for the glamorous couple. The judge, Arnaz, Ball, and their witnesses trooped to a nearby country club, where the ceremony took place in front of a crackling fireplace and a window overlooking snowy pines.

By the time they returned to the city, Arnaz was so late for his first show that the theater's management had been forced to explain the situation to an impatient audience. Then, when the couple walked onstage, a crowd of seven thousand stood and cheered.

The honeymoon consisted of their return train trip to California. Arnaz booked two compartments and joined them together to form a bridal suite. Always a romantic, he also filled them with red and white carnations, Ball's favorite flowers.

The newlyweds briefly lived in Ball's apartment, but informal country life appealed to both. They decided to find a place away from the city and bought a five-acre *ranchito* ("little ranch" in Spanish) near the town of Chatsworth. The area, in the San Fernando Valley about thirty miles from RKO Studios, was then sparsely populated, and their new home was surrounded mainly by orange and fig groves. It was considered, Ball recalled, "the wild and woolly open space then, and many movie people built homes there to get away from it all."[36]

After eloping to Connecticut, Arnaz carries Ball over the threshold into his dressing room at the Roxy Theater in New York.

THE *RANCHITO*

They loved their place and spent hours remodeling and redecorating it themselves. They planted a large garden. Arnaz built a brick barbeque and a guest house (where he slept when they had fights). Ball collected china and antique furniture, tended the garden, and fed the chickens, dogs, and other animals. After rejecting several possible combinations of their names to call the ranch, including Ludes and Arball, they settled on Desilu.

Weekends often found them hosting parties for their Hollywood friends.

Hours were devoted to Ball's passion for games such as cards and charades, and guests consumed quantities of Arnaz's cooking, especially his Cuban black beans and rice with chicken. Their daughter, Lucie, wrote that the couple's years on the ranch "with its livestock, its dogs and cats, fruit and vegetable gardens and all the refurbishing projects were the most idyllic in their lives together."[37]

However, more cracks were beginning to appear in the relationship, in addition to their ongoing jealous quarrels. Much of the problem centered on Arnaz's perception that his wife's career was moving forward

Yearning for a more rural lifestyle, Ball and Arnaz bought a five-acre ranch outside of Los Angeles. Here, they relax at home with their dogs in 1942.

LEAVING IN SPIRIT

This excerpt from Kathleen Brady's Lucille: The Life of Lucille Ball *indicates how much Ball was in love with Arnaz during the early years of their marriage:*

"She was completely and obviously besotted with her new husband. When Desi went to the studio's barber, she supervised his haircut from a perch in the bootblack's chair. A writer from *Collier's* magazine noted an amazing phenomenon: 'The procedure is this: you start interviewing Miss Lucille Ball and then Mr. Desi Arnaz enters and Miss Ball leaves. It is not that she leaves in person, she merely leaves in spirit. . . . Miss Lucille Ball looked at Mr. Desi Arnaz as if he were something that had floated down from above on a cloud.'"

Ball was very much taken with Arnaz from their first meeting. She claimed she fell in love with him "in about five minutes."

while his was not. His movies subsequent to *Too Many Girls* had been poorly received, and he resented the fact that people recognized his wife but not him. Furthermore, he worried that people dismissed him as an unknown no-talent taking advantage of his wife's success. He wanted to do what he had done before with success—take a band out on the road—but Ball urged him to stay. Frustrated, he often made remarks like, "There's no way I'm going to stay here and become Mr. Ball!"[38]

THE "LUCY LOOK" IS BORN

Ball's time at RKO, meanwhile, was ending. One of her last films there was *The Big Street*, an unusual drama about a bitter, wheelchair-bound woman who abuses the friendship of an adoring busboy. Ball always considered it her favorite of all the films she made, but it flopped. The movie's failure to click with audiences prompted RKO to sell Ball's contract to MGM.

She was delighted. MGM was a prestigious studio with a reputation for high-quality movies. Furthermore, the studio's head, Louis B. Mayer, liked and supported her. Wanting to emphasize her roles in comedy, Mayer first cast her as the lead in *DuBarry Was a Lady*, his version of Cole Porter's smash Broadway musical. Despite its faults—it cut most of Porter's songs and today seems slow and dated—the movie was a hit. Ball was such a poor singer that her musical numbers had to be dubbed by a professional.

Historically, *DuBarry* is notable because it marked the beginning of Ball's soon-to-

be-famous "Lucy look." Her hair was dyed red for the first time. Also, her eyebrows, lashes, and lips were emphasized. She would maintain the look for the rest of her life.

ALMOST DIVORCED

America's entry into World War II disrupted Ball and Arnaz's new marriage, as it disrupted the lives of millions of others. Arnaz was initially away for months with the Hollywood Victory Caravan, a trainload of stars and musicians that crisscrossed the country to benefit the Army and Navy Relief Fund. Then, in 1943, soon after being granted U.S. citizenship, he was drafted.

The musician was assigned to bombardier school, but he damaged his knee and was reassigned to noncombat duty, teaching English to illiterate draftees. His base was only fifteen minutes from Chatsworth, but he rarely made it home even when he had a weekend pass. Arnaz and Ball saw less and less of each other as the war progressed.

Ball suspected that he was using the weekends for affairs. In desperation, feeling that the marriage was slipping away, Ball filed for divorce in 1944. She admitted to reporters that her husband had always stayed away for days at a time, even before his military duties kept him away. She told gossip columnist Louella Parsons, however, that she did not blame him entirely: "I'm just as much to blame as Desi. We both have tempers and we're both difficult when we are battling."[39]

Before the divorce became final, however, the couple reconciled. Arnaz promised to spend more time at home, and both resolved to keep arguments from escalating. Asked by a reporter what adjustments he had made in order to achieve the reconciliation, Arnaz claimed he could name only two: sleeping with the windows open, which Ball preferred, and taking up square dancing.

FREELANCING

The couple's reconciliation and the end of Arnaz's military service in 1945 did not solve all of Ball's difficulties. MGM's executives were beginning to lose faith in her, despite a string of hits she made for them; they felt she was too ordinary and not glamorous enough. They began pressuring her to appear in mediocre pictures, hoping she would break her contract and save them money.

During this period, Ball suffered a three-month period of depression and withdrawal. With Arnaz out of town touring with his band, she spent most of her time at home, alone and tearful. Ball snapped out of this "mini-breakdown" (as she later called it) when an agent, Kurt Frings, convinced her to fight the studio. Earlier Frings

Ball (second from left) in DuBarry Was a Lady, *where she debuted her trademark "Lucy look."*

had successfully helped actress Olivia de Havilland with a similar situation. Ball was successful in facing down the studio and made only a few more films for it before her contract elapsed in 1946; she hired Frings in place of her old agent.

For the next three years, Ball was a freelancer, making movies for other studios (including *Sorrowful Jones* with Bob Hope) and dabbling in radio appearances and touring theater (where she starred in a well-received play, *Dream Girl*). She needed to keep working: Arnaz's band was successful, but he had racked up thousands of dollars in debt, mostly in gambling debts and back taxes. Ball was happy to help him pay back these debts, and Arnaz let her, but the bandleader was proud. Careful to avoid the stereotype of the Latin lover who takes advantage of women, he always considered her money a loan and kept strict accounts of how he repaid it.

RADIO

Ball signed again with Columbia Studios in 1949. Her first films there were two popular screwball comedies, both excellent: *Miss Grant Takes Richmond*, about a wacky secretary who gets involved with crooks, and *The Fuller Brush Girl*, about a wacky door-to-door saleswoman who gets involved with crooks. The trade newspaper *Variety* loved the latter, calling it a "rollicking, slam-bang, slapstick comedy with Lucille Ball at her very best."[40]

DIFFERENT BACKGROUNDS

In her memoir, Love, Lucy, *Ball comments on how vastly different she and Arnaz were in their upbringings and backgrounds:*

"Our outlooks on life were very different. Desi's family ranches stretched as far as he could ride a horse in a day. I was raised in a little white house near the railroad tracks and an amusement park; I never even owned a bicycle as a kid. When Desi was fifteen, he was living like a young prince, with cars and speedboats and horses; I was looking for a penny to make subway fare in New York.

Desi was raised with the idea that the man's word is law; he makes all the decisions; God made woman only to bear children and run the home. I wanted a masterful husband, God knows – and part of me wanted to be cherished and cared for. But all my life I'd been taught to be strong and self-reliant and independent, and I wondered if I could change."

Ball's role in The Fuller Brush Girl *(pictured) showcased her comedic abilities, and critics praised it as "Lucille Ball at her very best."*

The most important development in Ball's career, however, came from a different medium: radio. The actress had appeared periodically on radio throughout the 1940s, and she loved it. She blossomed in front of audiences, which radio shows typically had, because they responded immediately to her comedy. As she once remarked, this instant feedback was crucial to timing her lines and delivering gags: "I am a real ham. I love an audience. . . . I am dead, in fact, without one."[41]

Despite her love of the medium and experience with it, not until the end of the 1940s did Ball begin a regular radio show. Another agent who worked in Frings' office—Don Sharpe—specialized in assembling, or "packaging," radio shows for established movie stars. With her permission, he approached the CBS Radio

Network with an idea for casting her in a show about the scatterbrained wife of a rising banking executive.

CBS liked the idea, and an audition (a sample episode, now called pilots) called *Mr. and Mrs. Cugat* aired in the summer of 1948, costarring Lee Bowman. By the time it became a regular series in the fall, Richard Denning had replaced Bowman, the Cugats became Liz and George Cooper, and the title was *My Favorite Husband*. Rounding out the regular cast were Gale Gordon and Bea Benaderet, as Cooper's boss and his wife.

My Favorite Husband remained on the air until 1951. Much of its success can be credited to its talented writing team: a young couple, Bob Carroll Jr. and Madelyn Pugh, and a seasoned veteran, Jess Oppenheimer. Together with Ball—who felt free to provide input now that she was the star of her own show—the writers created a character and a premise that were the direct ancestors of Lucy Ricardo and *I Love Lucy*.

TV ARRIVES

Ball's years as the star of a hit radio show coincided with the decline of the medium as a dominant form of entertainment. A new, fascinating, untested medium was moving in on both radio and movies. Television appeared to many to be the wave of the future, and a number of celebrities—including Jack Benny, Milton Berle, and the team of George Burns and Gracie Allen—were defecting to it.

The proof, they felt, was in the numbers. In 1947 only 179,000 TV sets were

(Left to right) Madelyn Pugh, Jess Oppenheimer, and Bob Carroll Jr. wrote for Ball's radio show My Favorite Husband.

bought in America. Two years later that number had skyrocketed to more than 2 million. In those cities that had TV stations, the numbers of people who habitually went to see movies, nightclub shows, and sporting events were dropping drastically. Even restaurants were experiencing a slump, as millions of people stayed home to eat dinner in front of the TV.

There were only three major networks and two small ones. Broadcasts were in black and white, reception was notoriously poor, and the standard screen size was only ten inches. Nonetheless, TV was an amazing and exciting phenomenon. Entire neighborhoods crowded nightly into those few homes that boasted TV sets, eagerly watching the miracle of live pictures being sent across the country.

Movie and radio executives were naturally terrified of TV, seeing it as an enemy bent on stealing their audiences. At first many studios forbade their actors from appearing on television, unless they were directly promoting a film. As time went on, however, movie and radio executives decided to fight back. One obvious solution was to transfer proven successes to TV, something the CBS Radio executives were eager to do with *My Favorite Husband*.

DEVELOPING THE SHOW

Ball was reluctant. She feared that prolonged exposure on television might end her movie career. On the other hand, she saw it as an opportunity to work with her husband. Ball had long been interested in doing this, if only to keep Arnaz's wanderings from home to a minimum. Fearing that his constant touring was driving them apart, she told a friend, "If he goes on the road, I'll either travel with him or I'll lose him."[42]

Arnaz, for his part, was immediately enthusiastic. He liked television and sensed its potential. Unlike his wife, he had no thriving movie career to worry about. Furthermore, he was eager to stop traveling because he wanted to start a family.

CBS's plan was to directly transfer *My Favorite Husband* to TV. Ball, however, disagreed. She wanted to develop a different show—and she insisted on using Arnaz in the role of her husband. CBS was wary of this idea. The executives worried that the public would not accept them as a couple—a typical American redhead married to a foreign-born bandleader whose command of the language was so eccentric that a sign in his dressing room read "English Broken Here." Ball later commented that the CBS executives also worried that Arnaz was an artistic lightweight: "They thought Desi was just a bongo player."[43]

Undeterred, Ball and Arnaz formed Desilu Productions and set about developing their show, a thinly disguised version of their own life together. Ball later joked about this similarity to real life, "We decided that instead of divorce lawyers profiting from our mistakes, we'd profit from them."[44]

TV BOUND

The couple concocted a scheme to convince CBS that the combination of Arnaz and Ball would work with the American public. They created a live show that combined comedy routines by the pair with music by Arnaz and his orchestra.

Don Sharpe, the agent who had helped Ball establish herself on radio, booked a cross-country string of appearances for them during the summer of 1950. They appeared primarily in movie houses, performing before the feature film. The shows received rave reviews and played

"THE ONLY BONE OF CONTENTION"

Jess Oppenheimer, the longtime head writer for I Love Lucy, *formally registered the concept for the show with the Screenwriters Guild when it was still just an idea. His concept is reprinted in Coyne Steven Sanders and Tom Gilbert's* Desilu: The Story of Lucille Ball and Desi Arnaz:

"He is a Latin-American orchestra leader and singer. She is his wife. They are happily married and very much in love. The only bone of contention between them is her desire to get into show business and his equally strong desire to keep her out of it. As show business is the only way he knows to make a living, and he makes a very good one, the closest he can get to his dream is having a wife who's out of show business and devotes herself to keeping as nearly a normal life as possible for him."

to packed audiences. Unfortunately, the tour had to be cut short when the couple experienced a personal tragedy: finally pregnant after years of trying, Ball suffered a miscarriage.

The enthusiastic response by audiences to the tour convinced CBS, and the network gave the couple the go-ahead to produce an audition pilot. Ball and Arnaz enlisted *My Favorite Husband*'s writing team, and—though they had no idea at the time of its impact—they began the process of creating a series that would change the course of television.

Chapter

4 The Glory Years

"I was part of the beginning, when TV was a lot easier and a lot more fun, especially when none of us knew what we were doing. To watch it come out all right was great."

—Lucille Ball

No one, of course, knew how successful the series would be—or even if it would be successful at all. Ball had no great expectations for it. She thought it would be a fun thing to do for perhaps a season or two.

According to Ball, the title of the series came from a comment Arnaz made while they were fleshing out her character. "She tries so hard . . . she can't dance and she can't sing . . . she's earnest and pathetic . . . Oh, I love that Lucy!"[45] Someone suggested using *I Love Lucy* for the show's title, and Ball liked it for several reasons. "People would know that the 'I' was Desi. That gave him first billing. And then, how could you go wrong with the word 'love' in the title?"[46]

PULLING TOGETHER THE TEAM

CBS had difficulty finding a sponsor for the show; many potential clients had reservations about Arnaz. Eventually, however, the Philip Morris tobacco company agreed to underwrite it. Because the show was new and untested, Philip Morris got a bargain: they paid $23,500 per episode, less than half what top shows of the time cost.

Company executives laid down several conditions for their support. Chief among these concerned Arnaz and his music. They wanted his involvement kept to a minimum, and only after the show was a smash and he had proven his popularity with audiences did they relent. (Philip Morris exercised its authority in other ways as well. Ball smoked Chesterfields, a rival brand. On the set, she had to carry her cigarettes in a Philip Morris box, in case representatives of her sponsor happened by.)

Meanwhile, Ball and Arnaz leased studio space in a bare-bones building called the General Services Studio and began recruiting employees. In addition to their proven writing team, they approached another old pro, semiretired cameraman Karl Freund, about overseeing the camera work and lighting. Freund had worked with Ball at MGM, and she liked and trusted him.

THE GLORY YEARS ■ 55

An Academy Award winner, "Papa" Freund was already wealthy, and the salary Desilu could pay him was not an enticement. However, Arnaz guessed correctly that the veteran cameraman would not be able to resist the show's many technical challenges: "The challenge was what got him, and that's what I was counting on."[47]

FINDING FRED AND ETHEL

Ball's first choices to play her onscreen friends and neighbors Fred and Ethel Mertz were her costars from *My Favorite Husband*, Gale Gordon and Bea Benaderet. Unfortunately, both actors had already agreed to appear on other TV shows by the time *I Love Lucy* was approved. Their places were filled by Vivian Vance and William Frawley. Ball initially vetoed the choice of Vance, with whom she had never worked. For one thing, Ball thought of the Mertzes as older and dumpy, which Vance was definitely not. She was an attractive, svelte, and accomplished actress two years younger than Ball.

Vance was eager to get the role, however, and convinced Ball that she could "play dumpy." She was approved for the part—but Ball, always careful to remain the best-looking woman on the set, made sure her costar remained dumpy. Vance's contract contained a clause stipulating that she was required to be twenty pounds overweight during the filming season.

The network, for its part, initially disapproved of the choice of stocky ex-vaudevillian Frawley as Fred Mertz. He had long had a reputation as an unreliable alcoholic. However, Arnaz made him a rigorous deal: Frawley would get the job, but he would be fired the first time he missed a shoot or showed up drunk. Arnaz, who was always disciplined about work despite his own fondness for alcohol, recalled that Frawley held to the bargain: "He never missed a day's work, nor was he even a few minutes late during all the years he was with us."[48]

THE FIRST BABY

In the fall of 1950, just before *I Love Lucy* was due to begin shooting, Ball discovered that she was pregnant again. "For ten years," the comedian wrote in her memoir, "Desi and I had been trying to become costars and parents; now our dearest goals were being realized much too fast. We suddenly felt unprepared for either and began to have second thoughts."[49]

Arnaz and Ball considered scrapping the show but in the end decided to continue. Ball was determined to keep working as long as possible. As her due date—and the date of the first shoot—came closer, she became a bundle of restless energy. At one point, desperate to work off nervous energy, she enlisted Vance to help her clean the bathrooms in Desilu's rented studios.

Rehearsals and preparations continued, although the shooting was delayed until the birth of Ball's baby. Stagehand Barney McNulty recalled that everyone was concerned about the star's pregnancy and how it might affect the production: "We crossed our fingers, but she was a rare combination of nervousness and effectiveness."[50]

Vivian Vance and William Frawley were cast as the Ricardos' neighbors Fred and Ethel Mertz.

Lucie Arnaz was born on July 17, 1951. (Ball had chosen the name Susan, but Arnaz put "Lucie" on the birth certificate to surprise his wife.) The birth was a difficult one, with the baby's head coming out last in a breech birth, and an emergency operation called a cesarean, or C-section, had to be performed.

Ball, ecstatic at the birth of her child, spent six weeks at home with Lucie. She then went back to work.

TECHNICAL CHALLENGES

Developing the show, casting, and scheduling around Ball's pregnancy created only some of the problems Arnaz and Ball faced. The show's technical challenges were also formidable. Television was so new in the 1950s that many of the procedures that are now standard were still untested and unformed; the *I Love Lucy* crew needed to create its own way of doing things.

Some of the problems arose because Ball and Arnaz decided to film in front of a live audience, making *I Love Lucy* the first situation comedy to be shot in that way. They knew that live audiences would be essential to the show's success because Ball understood the importance of playing off an audience's reactions. Years later she remarked, "An audience gives you an instant barometer. . . . It's a great feeling."[51]

Ball, Arnaz, and their daughter Lucie, who was born on July 17, 1951.

However, including a live audience—then a relatively rare occurrence for TV—created problems. For one thing, the Desilu crew needed to keep curious audience members, unused to a TV studio, from wandering onto the set. A more serious problem was to ensure that the audience's view was not blocked while moving the bulky cameras around the set.

Still more technical challenges arose because Ball and Arnaz insisted on shooting the series in Hollywood, not in New York City, where most TV shows were then produced. Since California is in an earlier time zone, this prohibited broadcasting live (as was the norm) and still remaining in prime time across the country.

MULTICAMS

The Desilu team solved this problem with a novel solution that is now standard operating procedure: they recorded on film, then edited the footage for later broadcast. The program could then be broadcast nationally at the same time in each time zone. This method was far more expensive and time-consuming than live broadcasts, and CBS agreed to the extra expense only when Arnaz and Ball offered to take substantial salary cuts. *I Love Lucy* was not the first sitcom to be shot on movie film and edited later; that honor belongs to *Amos 'n' Andy*. However, the show's success helped popularize the technique, and it set the standard for future productions.

Still another innovation was the use of multiple cameras. Freund and his crew decided to use three cameras, instead of the single unit then standard for most live broadcasts. This technique, called multicam, had been pioneered by the game show *Truth or Consequences* in the late 1940s, but it had never before been used for a situation comedy.

The use of multicam improved the show's quality immensely. By shooting with multicam and editing, Desilu could utilize to the fullest the presence of a live

A view of the I Love Lucy *set shows the three cameras the crew utilized.* I Love Lucy *was the first sitcom to use this multicam technique.*

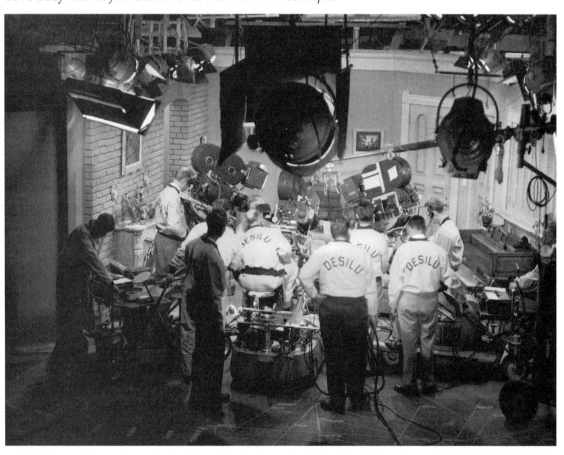

audience and the talents of the actors, timing reaction shots, double takes, and other actors' devices to the split second. The result was a far more sophisticated production than any television comedy or drama to date.

Furthermore, the use of movie film created a high-quality record of the show. The standard recording in the TV industry until then had been with a crude, poor-quality system called kinescope, which Ball recalled was "about as sharp as a piece of cheesecloth."[52] Creating a high-quality tape was essential for broadcasting and rebroadcasting—and with this decision Desilu paved the way for its pioneering use of syndication in later years.

A Hit

After more than a year of preparation, *I Love Lucy* debuted on Monday, October 15, 1951, at 9 P.M. The first show that was shot required substantial editing, so the first episode broadcast was actually the second one shot. It was called "The Girls Want to Go to a Nightclub."

Ball and Arnaz in a still from an early episode of I Love Lucy. *The show first aired on October 15, 1951.*

In this excerpt from a 1986 interview, "Lucy Has Grown Up a Lot," U.S. News & World Report, *Ball comments on the suddenness of her fame following the success of* I Love Lucy *(the tour she refers to was for promotional appearances):*

"I remember when we took our first tour and saw how people reacted. We'd made an instant, into-their-living-room connection. The closeness with the audience was unbelievable. I'd been in pictures for 12 years or more and made 40 or 50, and most people hardly knew who I was. Then after three months on TV, everybody in the country knew us and felt so close to us. That has never changed."

Not everyone loved it. The president of Philip Morris found the show "unfunny, silly, and totally boring."[53] Critics generally thought the writing was lifeless. However, the critics almost unanimously praised Ball. Typical was the reaction of the trade paper *Hollywood Reporter*: "The outstanding pertinent fact about *I Love Lucy* is the emergence, long suspected, of Lucille Ball as America's number-one comedienne. She is a consummate artist, born for the television."[54]

The public was less ambiguous than the critics. They loved *I Love Lucy*. The show was an instant hit. Within a month it was in the top ten, and by early 1952 it was the number-one show on the air. The show's popularity hardly wavered in the following years. For four out of its six seasons, *I Love Lucy* remained the number-one show on television. (It was narrowly edged out by a game show, *The $64,000 Question*, when not on top.) At its peak, during the 1952–53 season, it averaged a 67.3 rating, meaning that on a typical Monday night, more than two-thirds of all homes with TV sets were watching Lucy.

I Love Lucy's phenomenal success affected American life in unexpected ways. In cities that had television stations, for instance, telephone and water usage dropped significantly on Monday evenings during its time slot. People were glued to their televisions, and they avoided making phone calls or going to the bathroom.

THE SHOWS

Lucy's basic premise stayed constant over the years, but the characters and their relationships deepened. Ditsy, showbiz-crazy, trouble-prone Lucy was balanced by Ricky's mixture of self-confidence, affectionate condescension, and slow-burning frustration. Added to these were the Mertzes—gruff Fred and nosy Ethel—who bickered constantly and sometimes supported, sometimes opposed the Ricardos and their antics.

For their millions of fans, tuning in to this foursome was like seeing old friends. As the years went by, furthermore, the changes in the characters' lives mirrored those of millions of Americans in the increasingly affluent '50s. The Ricardos acquired a television set and a washing machine, started a family, made a pilgrimage to Hollywood, and moved to the suburbs.

I Love Lucy maintained its focus on these main characters. However, many episodes also featured famous guests. Orson Welles, Rock Hudson, William Holden, Richard Widmark, Tallulah Bankhead, and John Wayne were only a few of the celebrities who showed up on the show, often playing themselves.

Every *Lucy* fan has his or her favorite episodes. Many of these plots were inspired by incidents in Ball's own life. When the writers discovered that she refused to kill any of the chickens on her Chatsworth ranch, for instance, they worked it into a script. Writer Bob Carroll commented, "When we learned she had played the saxophone as a child, we used that. When she went back to her high school reunion— also used. Anything was fair game."[55]

In one memorable show, Lucy and Ethel get jobs wrapping candy in a chocolate factory. The candy shoots by on a conveyor belt too fast, however, and as the pair fall behind in their work, they try to keep pace by stuffing candies into their mouths. In another, while the four are on vacation in Italy, Lucy is invited to play a role in an upcoming Italian film called *Bitter Grapes*. Thinking (wrongly) that the movie will be about the wine industry, she tries to soak up local color by stomping grapes in a vineyard—and so loses her chance to be in the movie.

In another, while trying to imitate a pioneer woman, Lucy opens her oven to remove freshly baked bread and is pinned against the sink by an enormous, monstrously growing loaf. Yet another classic episode finds her appearing in a commercial for a health tonic called Vitameatavegamin. Not knowing that the medicine is highly alcoholic, Lucy swigs more and more with each take and unwittingly gets drunk.

LUCY GETS PREGNANT

The episodes that form perhaps the show's most famous sequences mirrored a real-life occurrence: Ball's pregnancy and the birth of her second child. Ball and Arnaz were thrilled when she became pregnant in the spring of 1952, even though at first it looked as though it would have disastrous consequences for the show.

When she discovered that she was expecting, Ball's writers were delighted with the plot possibilities. Ball was worried, however, and with good reason. Within the movie studio system she was familiar with, pregnant actresses were routinely suspended until they gave birth. Ball had no guarantee that CBS would not pull the plug on *I Love Lucy* when they found out.

The executives at CBS and Philip Morris were indeed concerned. In the buttoned-down '50s, even showing a double bed in a married couple's bedroom was considered too risqué for TV. Philip Morris's advertising agency flatly refused to let a pregnant woman be shown on television. Some executives suggested a compromise, with Ball filmed only when standing behind chairs or otherwise blocked from view.

However, Ball and Arnaz held their ground, knowing that they wielded a certain amount of clout. After all, they had the top show on television, with an average audience of 31 million. They insisted that Ball's pregnancy be written into the show. Arnaz wrote a long and heartfelt letter to Philip Morris explaining the situation, asking in veiled language if the tobacco company really wanted to walk away from its lucrative deal with Desilu, and Philip Morris relented.

Even after this, the sponsor and network insisted on certain precautions. The show's writers were forbidden to use the word

Ball in the popular episode "Lucy Does a TV Commercial," in which she drinks the alcoholic health tonic Vitameatavegamin.

pregnant, and the less offensive *expectant* was substituted. A rabbi, a priest, and a Protestant minister reviewed each episode for possible vulgarities. This committee, Ball recalled in her memoir, never found any problems; on the contrary, she said, the committee was "heartily in favor of what we were doing: showing motherhood as a happy, wholesome, normal family event."[56]

"MAN, IT WAS BEDLAM!"

Right up until the last moment, the writers prepared shows reflecting the impending birth. When it arrived, the comedian's sense of timing was, as usual, perfect.

Since the birth of Ball's first child had required a C-section, the second was performed the same way. Such operations can generally be scheduled in advance, and Ball's was performed on the morning of the same Monday when her television counterpart would give birth. As a result, Lucille Ball gave birth to Desi Arnaz Jr. on January 19, 1953. Lucy Ricardo gave birth to Ricky Ricardo Jr. that evening. The former was a joy for the Arnaz family; the latter was brilliant television. In his memoir, Arnaz called it "the most unbelievable piece of timing I know of."[57]

The public's anticipation of the birth was frenzied. Newspaper columnists (fed by news flashes from Desilu's publicity office) speculated for weeks about the sex of the baby. Just before the due date, impatience reached a fever pitch; the show's public relations director recalled: "All day

SHE KNEW IT COULD BE DONE

Madelyn Pugh, long a part of Ball's writing team, discusses her boss's attitude toward writers. The passage is from Charles Hingham's Lucy: The Real Life of Lucille Ball:

"When Lucy first met you, she tended to be a bit wary, a little challenging. But once you convinced her you knew what you were doing, she would trust your ideas all the way. Some of the stunts we wrote for her could have been dangerous. Yet never once did Lucy back off from any of them, although Desi frequently wanted her to because he was concerned for her safety.

She trusted us enough to know that Bob and I had worked out every piece of business ourselves beforehand to make sure it *could* be done. If Lucy had to climb onto a barrel, say, then she'd know it was possible because we'd done it ourselves. . . . If the script called for her to hide dozens of uncooked eggs inside her dress, she knew that I'd tried it myself first to see if it was possible and if it was funny."

Ball holds her infant son Desi Arnaz Jr. while his sister Lucie looks on. The much-anticipated birth occurred on January 19, 1953.

Friday, Saturday, and Sunday I was trapped at my telephone. Newspapers ran hourly bulletins, they ran pools betting on the baby's sex, you couldn't turn on your radio without hearing the question would it be a boy or a girl. Man, it was bedlam!"[58]

Arnaz and Ball had instructed their writers to make their television child a boy, no matter what the real baby's sex was. Ball remarked that there were two reasons for this. One was that Arnaz desperately wanted a boy to carry on the family name. The other was simply consideration for their daughter: "We had a very precocious two-year-old girl on our hands, and if the Ricardo baby was a girl, then Lucie would never understand why it wasn't her. It was just best for everybody that it was a boy."[59]

"LOVE AND KISSES FROM ALL AMERICA"

For nine months Lucy Ricardo's vast audience had faithfully followed her pregnancy. On the night she finally gave birth, some 44 million people tuned in—a larger audience than the one that watched the next day as Dwight Eisenhower took the oath of office as president of the United States.

On the show Ricky, Fred, and Ethel carefully rehearse getting Lucy to the hospital. When the time comes, however, they become so excited that they rush off and almost forget her. At the end of the show, over a shot of a newborn baby, an announcer intoned, "May their lives together be filled with as much joy and laughter and carefree happiness as they have brought all of us week after week. To Lucy, to Ricky, and to the new baby: love and kisses from Philip Morris and from all America."[60]

The arrival of Desiderio Alberto Arnaz IV was trumpeted around the world within minutes. *I Love Lucy* was a hit in Europe, South America, and parts of Asia, and fans were just as eager there for news as in America. Informed that the Arnaz baby was a boy, just as he had written for the show, Jess Oppenheimer exclaimed, "Terrific! That makes me the greatest writer in the world. Tell Lucy she can have the rest of the day off!"[61]

In the next weeks, the new mother was honored everywhere. She was featured on the covers of *Look*, *Life*, and *Newsweek* magazines. The public inundated her with thousands of cards, and so many flowers that they filled two floors of the

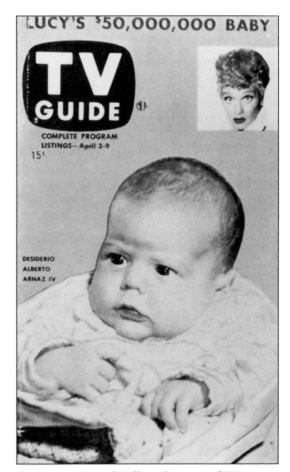

Desi Arnaz Jr. and Ball on the cover of TV Guide, *one of the many periodicals that featured stories about the birth.*

hospital. She and her show won several Emmys at that year's ceremonies, a display of approval she always attributed, at least in part, to sentimentality over the birth of her child.

THE HUAC SCARE

The birth of her son proved that Lucy Ricardo had a firm grasp on America's affection, but an incident that occurred around the same time came close to wrecking her career. It came about because a casual promise made to her grandfather decades earlier returned to haunt her.

In 1936 her grandfather Fred Hunt, a socialist, had insisted that Ball and other family members register as members of the Communist Party. She dutifully registered and promptly forgot about it. Then, when the so-called Red Scare gripped America in the early 1950s, this forgotten act surfaced.

The Red Scare, an outgrowth of the cold war between the United States and the communist Soviet Union, was perpetrated by right-wing, conservative politicians and leaders determined to root out suspected left-wing infiltrators in powerful areas such as Hollywood and the government. It was a terrifying time for many people; even simply being accused of communist sympathies, with nothing proven, was enough to taint a career forever.

One of the most vigorous bodies investigating alleged communists was a branch of Congress, the House Un-American Activities Committee (HUAC). When HUAC discovered Ball had once registered as a communist, she was summoned to testify in April 1952. Ball explained that she had done it only to placate her grandfather, whom the family called Daddy. "We did it to please Daddy," she recalled. "He'd had one stroke already and the least little argument got him all upset."[62]

The HUAC representatives accepted her explanation. The following year, however—when public interest in Ball's baby was at a fever pitch and she and Arnaz were in the midst of signing lucrative movie and TV deals—she again was investigated by publicity-hungry members of HUAC.

Once again Ball appeared before Republican congressmen in Los Angeles, in the company of her mother and brother. She repeated her earlier testimony, adding, "I have never been too civic-minded and certainly never political-minded in my life."[63] The congressmen again cleared her of suspicion and promised that her appearance before them would be kept secret.

THE NEWS BREAKS

It was not kept secret, however. Ball was at home a few days later when she heard radio commentator Walter Winchell announce on his national broadcast, "The top television comedienne has been confronted with her membership in the Communist Party!"[64]

Within a few days, the *Los Angeles Herald-Express* published a misleading copy of Ball's registration card, cropped to leave off the expiration date of December 1938. Reporters dashed to cover this potentially scandalous story.

The new season was just starting, and the crew of *I Love Lucy* was almost too stunned to work. Ball was terrified on several fronts. First, she knew that if Philip Morris canceled its sponsorship of the show, it could mean the effective end of her career. More immediately, she feared that someone in the audience could attack her while taping the season's first

Ball's 1936 voter registration form, on which she affiliates herself with the Communist Party. Years later, this affiliation would be investigated by HUAC.

episode—or that the audience would, at the very least, boo her.

Arnaz decided that the best thing was to continue as usual—that not producing the show would be seen as a sign of weakness. However, he ordered extra security and had a doctor stand by during the filming of the first show, in case his nervous wife suffered problems. Vance later recalled, "I think that if Lucy had heard one boo from that audience, she'd have collapsed."[65] Arnaz even talked CBS into

canceling the show that was scheduled to come on after the next *I Love Lucy* would be broadcast. This would have let the couple go live nationally to tell their side of the story if needed.

They did not have to worry, however. Before the show was filmed, Arnaz did not deliver his usual lighthearted warm-up. Instead, he spoke seriously to the studio audience of three hundred, explaining how he and his wife felt and hoping for the audience's approval. He was rewarded with a huge burst of applause. When he introduced Ball, the crowd gave her a tremendous standing ovation.

That night Ball could do no wrong; the audience roared its approval of even the tiniest gesture. Afterward, Ball thanked them for their support before collapsing with relief backstage. To reporters in the following days, Arnaz maintained his light treatment of the affair, wisecracking, "The only thing that is red about this kid is her hair!"[66] The incident blew over quickly, and Ball's final vindication seemed to arrive when President Eisenhower invited the cast of *I Love Lucy* to perform at the White House later that year.

SLOWING DOWN SLIGHTLY

Inevitably, the personal lives of Ball and Arnaz began to change. Because of their show, they were famous and wealthy—and even busier than before. Added to this were the demands of their growing family. One major change was the decision to leave their beloved farm.

For years the couple had resisted when friends urged them to move to bigger or more prestigious property. However, after a kidnapping threat (apparently a hoax perpetrated by a mentally ill fan), they felt less secure living relatively far away from work. In addition, the area's increased population was making life there less appealing. They were sad to sell the *ranchito* but proud of the new home that Ball found for them—a handsome Beverly Hills mansion.

By the mid-1950s, Ball wanted to slow her work pace. She was tiring of grinding out a weekly series, and she wanted to end the show while it was still on top. In April 1957 she and Arnaz filmed the last episode of *I Love Lucy*, "The Ricardos Dedicate a Statue."

It was hardly in Ball's nature to retire, however. In the following years, she starred in a series of hour-long specials. She spent time with her children and indulged in her passion for games. She took on an increasingly active role in running the expanding Desilu Productions. And she dealt with a marriage that was crumbling.

5 The Nonstop Star

"Women's lib? I'm afraid it doesn't interest me one bit. I've been so liberated it hurts."

—Lucille Ball

On television Lucy Ricardo maintained her distinctively scatterbrained but lovable personality. In real life Lucille Ball was a much different person. She was complex, demanding, and often difficult. Ball's overriding personality trait may have been her need for constant work. A perfectionist and a taskmaster with herself, she insisted that colleagues maintain the same exacting standards. The star's nonstop energy and demanding nature, biographer Kathleen Brady has commented, set the pace for everyone else: "Most people needed to go to the bathroom, take a break, have a moment to themselves, but not Lucy, who drove her company on. Extrovert, star, and boss, she established the tone of the set."[67]

If a Desilu employee failed her somehow, she made her feelings plain, in clear and frank (and sometimes crude) language. Unlike her husband, who could charm and befriend nearly anyone, Ball had a brutal attitude unsoftened by social graces. According to Candy Moore, who played the actress's daughter on *The Lucy Show* in the 1960s, "She was very blunt and direct. She didn't have a sense of how to spare people while you're telling them what you need to tell them."[68]

DEALING WITH COLLEAGUES

This attitude was often intimidating. Ball could reduce even longtime colleagues like writer Madelyn Pugh to tears with her criticisms. Although Pugh, Carroll, and Oppenheimer had worked with Ball for years, the writing team dreaded the weekly script run-throughs.

Outright temper tantrums, however, were rare. Ball prided herself on her professionalism, and she tried hard not to let her ego get in the way of work. The star recalled that a psychiatrist had at one point helped her learn to control her feelings, rather than tactlessly blurting out what was on her mind: "She taught me how to rest in a roomful of people, to hold all my emotions in, instead of talking about them."[69]

Once a coworker had proven him- or herself, Ball generally maintained a cordial but brisk professional relationship.

Ball (left) with Vance, her costar and friend. The two had disputes but maintained a close relationship.

She rarely turned business ties into friendships. One exception was Vivian Vance, with whom she forged a complex, sisterlike, love-hate relationship. Vance was one of the few people associated with Desilu who dared to disagree with Ball, and she could hold her own in arguments with the star. Generally, though, Vance deferred to her boss, acknowledging that Ball had the power: "Okay, honey, you own the store. It's all right with me."[70]

Ball had a more amiable relationship with the testy Bill Frawley. Unlike many on the Desilu set, she tolerated his heavy drinking, gruff manner, and general indifference toward the show's production.

The cast and crew of I Love Lucy, *including Ball (front row, center), flanked by Arnaz, Vance, and Frawley.*

She ignored Frawley's surly attitude toward Vance—he and Vance never got along well—and she let him get away with behavior no one else on the set would dare to try. For instance, he was so disinterested in any part of a script that did not concern him that he sometimes dozed off during rehearsals.

THE DESILU FAMILY

Despite generally maintaining only cordial relationships, Ball liked to think of her employees as a big family. As Desilu Pro-

ductions grew—at its peak it employed about two hundred people—she tried to make them feel included. The company's annual picnics, for instance, were legendary. Daughter Lucie Arnaz remembers them as "big family affairs with softball games, relay races and tons of food. Everyone had a great time, and probably no one more than Lucy and Desi."[71]

The star was also capable of unexpected generosity, such as creating gifts that required tremendous planning. One Christmas, for instance, she gave Vance a scrapbook entitled "This Is Your Life, Vivian Roberta Jones." (Jones was the actress's real name; Vance was a stage name.) By herself, Ball had assembled photos from Vance's childhood onward, a painstaking process that involved weeks of secretly telephoning relatives for contributions.

The star was also generous in praising her coworkers in public. She often told reporters that her only gift was being able to execute what the writing team had created: "We just took ordinary situations and exaggerated them. . . . It wasn't my genius. It was the genius of craftsmen behind the scenes."[72]

OUTBURSTS

Alternately, Ball could be cruel in private. Harriet McCain, her longtime personal maid, often bore the brunt of the star's temper—but McCain was not always intimidated.

Once, while Ball was sitting in a makeup chair, she demanded a glass of water. Someone gave it to McCain, who handed it to Ball. Ball saw it had ice cubes, which she did not want, and petulantly threw it in the maid's face. McCain rushed to get more water, then returned and threw it in her boss's face.

Ball knew she could be tactless and would apologize later for her outbursts or bad temper. She often remarked that she wished she could say things without being hurtful, the way Arnaz could. Her daughter comments, "She would use a defensive way of getting something across. Maybe she was just terrified of hurting someone's feelings, so she'd just crash on ahead and get it over with."[73]

CONSTANT REHEARSAL

Another aspect of Ball's character was her perfectionism when preparing a show. Although many of the routines on her shows appear improvised, each was practiced and perfected until it could be timed to the second. This relentless rehearsal honed the rhythm and pace of each joke, scene, and show. The smallest gag was subject to scrutiny. Ball once spent three hours practicing a tiny throwaway moment—the popping of a paper bag—by experimenting with various ways of blowing up different bags. Even her husband's outbursts of frustrated Spanish, which seem like rapid-fire improvisations, were timed, then written out and added to the final script.

Ball credited two veterans of the silent-film era with teaching her the importance of rehearsal. Comedian Buster Keaton and director Eddie Sedgwick, she recalled, were "the first people to really sit me down and teach me all about slapstick comedy. Attention to detail, that's what it's all about. If I had to work with grapes, a loaf of bread, a cup of coffee, whatever, I had to test them first to know what I was eating or drinking, how hot or cold it was, how it got there, how it would ride on the tray."[74]

Ball worked closely with her writers and in run-throughs with the other actors to revise scripts; once completed, it was set in stone. She almost never allowed anyone, including herself, to deviate from a finished script. A rare exception was a scene in which she was wearing a fake putty nose. The nose accidentally caught fire when another actor lit her cigarette,

BOYS AGAINST GIRLS

Biographer Kathleen Brady, in Lucille: The Life of Lucille Ball, *notes how the simple but effective premises of the plots of* I Love Lucy *had a timeless quality to them:*

"Her funny faces and pranks spiraling out of control were incomparable, but the show offered much more. It had great heart. *I Love Lucy* was a story not just of the war between the sexes, but of the love between friends. The Fred who denounces Lucy as a ditsy woman bristles when someone else dares to accuse her of being a crook (although for story purposes he is soon ready to call the police). The show employed basic and timeless dramatic devices—especially in its dependence on the opposition of the practical Cuban steadying the scatterbrained American—and it balanced temperaments in a way that harkened back to the "humors" of the Elizabethan stage: patient Ethel, volatile Ricky, stolid Fred, and flighty, airy Lucy—couple against couple, boys against the girls."

(Left to right) Vance, Frawley, Arnaz, and Ball on the set of I Love Lucy.

and Ball improvised by dunking it in a cup of coffee.

WORK, WORK, WORK

The comedian usually worked from 10 A.M. to 6 P.M. daily. On nights when she had dress rehearsals or the show was filmed, she did not hesitate to work well into the evening. Even on weekends at home, Ball was unable to relax for long. Often she tied a scarf around her hair and cleaned house alongside her help.

Ball never took naps, calling them "deadening." At one point she took up painting for relaxation—but preferred watercolors because she was too impatient to let oil paint dry. Her son recalls, "Even when we were very young, my mother was never really able to turn off from whatever it is that drives her to work. Ever since I can remember, she has talked about 'getting away,' and when she does, she's great—for about three weeks; then she has to get back to work."[75]

In addition to Ball's compulsion to work was another, perhaps connected, personality trait. The actress had a powerful reluctance to spend money. As with many others of her generation, both her need to work and her frugality were connected with having lived through difficult times.

Ball grew up poor, and then lived through the Great Depression. For such people, working long hours was the only way to survive and every dollar was hard won. It was perhaps natural to be conservative with money, afraid that it might disappear. In this regard, Ball was typical of her generation. Although she was wealthy, the comedian found it almost impossible to enjoy the benefits of money.

Rather than buy even moderately priced dresses from department stores, she had a Desilu dressmaker copy dresses from ads. She brought office supplies home from work and hoarded them away. When she learned that Desilu had an account at a nearby gas station, she demanded to know who got the trading stamps that came with fill-ups and reportedly wanted them for herself.

DOING BUSINESS

Ball's private life was closely intertwined with her professional life—especially her working relationship with her husband. As long as they had been a couple, Ball had publicly praised and supported her husband's business acumen. She recognized, in particular, his ability to spot industry trends long before more seasoned veterans could. William Paley, the longtime head of CBS, once remarked, "He was a real talent, and it wouldn't have come to the surface if it weren't for her persistence."[76]

As Desilu grew, Ball was happy to let Arnaz emerge as the star of the business. She certainly had her opinions, but generally she let him do the talking in business meetings. Martin Leeds, a Desilu executive, recalled, "You never heard her say much when Desi was around. He'd leave and she'd start talking."[77]

One reason Arnaz was good at business was that he easily understood figures and had a virtually photographic memory for

"DESILOOT"

In the aftermath of the TV birth of Ricky Ricardo Jr., several commercial spin-offs from the TV show were devised. A Lucy newspaper comic strip and Lucy comic books appeared. Stores across the country began carrying official Lucille Ball and Desi Arnaz clothing lines, as well as dolls, aprons, furniture, games, jewelry, and more. Such spin-offs led to jokes within the industry about "Desiloot"—the sudden influx of wealth these products brought. The windfall was the beginning of the income that would make Ball and Arnaz wealthy. Quoted in Coyne Steven Sanders and Tom Gilbert's *Desilu: The Story of Lucille Ball and Desi Arnaz*, Ball cracked, "It couldn't happen to a nicer pair of kids. I mean our two children, of course."

A Lucille Ball paper doll, one sample of the flood of merchandise the show spawned.

them. Leeds remarked, "I can spend a couple of days working on a cost sheet, and he'll read it and understand it in one minute flat. Six months later, if the cost of something has gone up, he'll quote that first cost sheet and will want to know what has happened. He doesn't miss a thing."[78]

The most dramatic example of Arnaz's business savvy concerned the ownership of *I Love Lucy* itself. In the early days of television, syndication—the practice of leasing episodes to stations for rebroadcasting—was almost unknown. Arnaz understood early on, however, that syndication had the potential to be extremely lucrative—and that ownership of a successful show was a gold mine.

Before *I Love Lucy* became a hit, Arnaz had been willing to accept lower pay for himself and Ball. One of the considerations he received in return for this was ownership of the shows. This foresight paid off brilliantly a few years after their original broadcasts, when Desilu sold the rights for 180 *Lucy* shows to CBS for $4.3 million.

GROWING

Arnaz's coup allowed Desilu Productions to grow by leaps and bounds. The company bought controlling interest in a large production facility, the Motion Picture Center, and expanded its employee base. Among the key people were another writing team, Bob Schiller and Bob Weiskopf, who joined Pugh and Carroll after the departure of head writer Jess Oppenheimer.

Within a few years, the studio was handling technical production for dozens of shows, renting its studio space to other production companies, producing hundreds of commercials, and turning out dozens of TV shows. Some of Desilu's programs were short-lived, but others have become popular classics. Among the more memorable series the studio developed and produced over the years are *Our Miss Brooks*, *The Untouchables*, *Mission: Impossible*, *The Andy Griffith Show*, and *Star Trek*.

This production side of Desilu was in full swing when Ball and Arnaz ended *I Love Lucy* in 1957, at the end of the show's sixth season. The company then produced a series of hour-long specials over the three years, called *The Lucille Ball–Desi Arnaz Show* and *The Lucy-Desi Comedy Hour*, starring the pair. These had much larger budgets than the original *Lucy* shows and featured such notable guest stars as Red Skelton, Fernando Lamas, Fred MacMurray, and Maurice Chevalier.

Late in 1957 Desilu made a quantum jump in size. It purchased RKO Studios, the movie studio where Ball and Arnaz had met seventeen years before. Once a major studio, RKO had lost money under the direction of the eccentric billionaire Howard Hughes, and Arnaz was able to negotiate a bargain price of about $6 million.

As a result, Desilu could grow to occupy thirty-five sound stages, more than even giant MGM. Desilu also had back lots totaling forty acres, housing such memorable sets as Tara, the Southern plantation from *Gone with the Wind*. Referring to the expanse and condition of the new acquisition, as well as to her hands-off policy during the negotiations to buy it, Ball joked, "*I'm* not the one who bought RKO—I'm the one trying to get it *dusted*!"[79]

About a year later, Arnaz took Desilu public—that is, he sold stock in the company. Ball and Arnaz each retained 25 percent of the stock. After paying off his gambling debts, Arnaz was able to keep less than $100,000 from this windfall. Ball, however, had no personal debts; she put her profit—roughly $2.5 million before taxes—into solid investments.

THE MARRIAGE FRAYS

Desilu Productions had been created so that Ball and Arnaz could spend more time together. Ball had hoped that doing so would help hold her marriage together. With the show's runaway success, the goal of spending more time together had been met. They worked together all day, every day. However, the couple paid a price for this togetherness. The strain of being constantly together in the pressure-cooker atmosphere of a top TV production company began to show. Lucie Arnaz recalled, "The more my parents worked and were away from my brother and me, the higher the level of stress and anxiety at home."[80]

In public the couple rarely argued. Writer Bob Weiskopf recalls, "There were never any knock-down-drag-out fights around the set. Desi was from an upper-

Ball and Arnaz sign the contract for the purchase of RKO Studios by Desilu Productions on December 11, 1957.

crust sort of society in Cuba. He was too well-mannered. He'd be the last person in the world to drag out the dirty linen in front of anybody."[81] At home, however, things were different. In the evenings Arnaz and Ball were exhausted and strained after working all day together; their fights were more common than ever, complete with curses and flying china, and sometimes within earshot of the children. These battles began to be increasingly violent; according to one story, Ball once knocked Arnaz out with a hammer during a fight at their home. Occasionally, they would now fight in front of other people; at one dinner party at their house, Arnaz reportedly hit his wife and split her lip.

Arnaz had always had a habit of staying away for days at a time, retreating to the guest house on the ranch, to the family's vacation home in Del Mar, or to a Hollywood hotel. Now, even if they were getting along, he continued to do so. The couple also frequently spent their weekends apart. Ball stayed at home while Arnaz spent his time gambling in Las Vegas or on his boat, where he fished with male friends and, Ball suspected, entertained female guests.

PROBLEMS FOR ARNAZ

Arnaz had come far in his life. In less than twenty years, he had risen from unknown young show-biz hopeful to top star—a great comic foil for his wife, a talented actor who could memorize a script in a single reading, a successful television producer, and the head of a major studio.

As a husband, Arnaz was less successful. Ball had always downplayed or turned a blind eye to his dalliances with other women. As the years went on, however, this became less possible to ignore. Martin Leeds, speaking of the studio's staff, remarked, "The problem we had with Desi was that we knew she knew, and that hurt."[82]

Arnaz felt that since he genuinely loved Ball, he should not be held responsible for seeing other women. Since most of his girlfriends were prostitutes, he argued, they did not "count." This attitude is perhaps typical for a male of his generation and upbringing. He often remarked, in his memoirs and in conversation, that he considered himself nothing more than an old-fashioned Latin.

By the end of the 1950s, another of Arnaz's problems, alcohol, was getting the better of him. He had always been an enthusiastic drinker, but now it began to affect his judgment. If Desilu executives had important matters to discuss with him, they did so before 10 A.M., when Arnaz would have the first drink of the day. Knowing that he was becoming less capable of making sound decisions, they also began keeping Ball abreast of upcoming or ongoing projects.

Arnaz had always been a trim athlete, but now his health was failing. Despite doctors' warnings, however, he refused to slow down. Along with his work at Desilu, Arnaz vigorously pursued several projects, including construction of a luxurious resort hotel and another house for his family in the desert community of Rancho Mirage.

DRIFTING APART

The strain of keeping the marriage intact found Ball seeking psychiatric help periodically, for herself and together with her husband. Unfortunately, neither she nor Arnaz stayed with this therapy for long. Ball found a longer-lasting form of help for herself in the teachings of, and her friendship with, Dr. Norman Vincent Peale. Peale was an inspirational religious leader whose 1952 book, *The Power of Positive Thinking*, had been a best-seller. It combined Christian theology with a psychological approach to heightened self-esteem.

As the pressures in her personal life mounted, Ball tried to maintain her public composure. Sometimes, though, her efforts failed. In May 1959 Ball appeared at a Kiwanis Club youth rally combating juvenile delinquency in Oklahoma City, Oklahoma. When only two thousand of an estimated crowd of fifteen thousand turned out, the actress angrily blamed the organizers and left without even getting out of her limousine. National headlines scolded Ball's petulant behavior severely.

Soon after this embarrassing incident, the family left on a six-week European vacation. Arnaz had wanted just the two of them to go, but Ball insisted on taking the children as well as her cousin Cleo and her husband, Ken Morgan. The trip was a disaster. The couple fought constantly, and the children were afraid of what might happen. Arnaz was bored, restless, and uncommunicative. As if things were not already bad enough, Ball tripped and broke a toe. She recalled, "When he [Arnaz] wasn't drinking, he spent most of his time

Norman Vincent Peale, a religious leader and author whose friendship gave Ball comfort as her marriage fell apart.

on the phone with the studio or checking the Del Mar racetrack, where his horses were running. I was completely disenchanted, bitter, and unforgiving . . . and the kids saw and heard way too much."[83]

After they returned home, the problems continued. The Beverly Hills police occasionally brought Arnaz home, saying they had picked him up drunk and were returning him before he could get into more serious trouble. Gossip magazines, meanwhile, were openly suggesting that the marriage was in grave trouble.

In September 1959 Arnaz was briefly jailed for public drunkenness, allegedly having just left a house of prostitution.

That same month he asked Ball for a divorce and moved out. He bought forty acres in rural Corona and moved there on his own. The couple then began the sad process of telling their children about the split and dividing their assets. They still cared for each other, and deep sadness, rather than anger or hate, was the prevailing emotion.

"It Marked the End"

On the day divorce papers were formally filed, Arnaz and Ball were filming one of their last hour-long specials. The script called for Arnaz to passionately kiss Ball, who was disguised as a mustached chauffeur. "When the scene arrived and the cameras closed in for that final embrace," Ball recalled, "we just looked at each other, and then Desi kissed me, and we both cried. It marked the end of so many things."[84]

On March 2, 1960, the two filmed a final special, the last time the television legends would appear onscreen together. Their divorce became final the next day. At the courthouse, Ball dutifully clowned for reporters, but she revealed more genuine feelings when one reporter asked how she felt: "Not good," she replied. "How should I feel?"[85]

In the settlement, Ball got the houses in Beverly Hills and Rancho Mirage. Arnaz got the Del Mar house and his land in Corona. Each retained their 25 percent of Desilu stock. They shared joint custody of the children.

The divorce was headline news worldwide: America's favorite couple was no longer a couple. Now it was Ball's responsibility to maintain her life and career alone.

6 The Marriage Ends, but the Shows Go On

"She never gave less than a full-out performance, all stops out."

—*Wildcat* director Michael Kidd

Ball's philosophy was that hard work was always the best solution to mending the broken parts of her life. Therefore, immediately after the divorce decree, she made a movie. *The Facts of Life*, costarring her old friend Bob Hope, was a sophisticated farce about adultery—relatively daring material, especially in light of Ball's recent and very public breakup with Arnaz.

While on the set, Ball suffered an accident, falling while climbing into a boat during shooting. She gashed her leg and face badly and was knocked out for several minutes. When she regained consciousness, the first thing Ball saw was Hope standing anxiously over her. Referring to the sponsor of his television show, she joked, "I hope the ambulance is a Chrysler."[86]

Although he was now Ball's ex-husband, Arnaz rushed to be with her at the hospital. She was glad to have him there, and when she was released, they and their children all stayed at their home in Del Mar so that she could recuperate. Arnaz and Ball both acknowledged to reporters

that they still cared deeply about each other.

BROADWAY BOUND

For some time Ball had been considering a new project: a Broadway musical. After thinking over several possibilities, she settled on *Wildcat*, the story of a woman struggling to succeed in the male-dominated world of wildcat (independent) oil production.

She was daunted but not scared off by the fact that she could not sing. (An encouraging sign was the example of Rex Harrison, another nonsinging actor, who had recently triumphed as Professor Henry Higgins in *My Fair Lady*.) "I'm terrified of the musical end of it," she admitted to reporters before the show opened. "But I have some good people who know I'm not a singer and will write accordingly. I'll be doing a lot of cavorting around while I'm singing—and maybe that will keep people from paying too much attention to the quality of my *voice*!"[87]

Her collaborators on the project were, indeed, top notch. The author of *Wildcat* was N. Richard Nash, a successful playwright, and the choreographer-director was Michael Kidd, already famous for his stagings of such hit musicals as *Guys and Dolls* and *Finian's Rainbow*. The songs, meanwhile, were to be written by the gifted team of Carolyn Leigh and Cy Coleman.

Desi Arnaz was invited to invest in and produce the show, and he readily accepted the role. As friends and family recognized, he was still emotionally attached to Ball. "He would do anything for her," daughter Lucie recalls, "even after they separated."[88]

WILDCAT OPENS

To prepare for the show, Ball and her children moved to New York City. As soon as she had leased an apartment on the top floor of a luxury building, she created a ruckus there. Furious that the building association's regulations forbade her children's nanny, who was black, from using the regular elevator, she made the humiliating regulation public and forced the tenants to change it.

In 1960 Ball starred in the Broadway musical Wildcat *(pictured), hoping that people would focus on her "cavorting around" and not her singing.*

Ball had hoped that a new project and a change of locale would help her cope with the trauma of divorce. However, in some ways it was worse. The stress of the breakup was compounded by the new stresses of relocating across the country and the still-bothersome injuries from her fall. Furthermore, she had to cope with the intense physical and mental requirements of preparing for a Broadway show, where she would be in front of an audience every night instead of once a week.

All this threatened to take a serious toll on Ball's mental and physical health, even

Ball in Wildcat. *Although the show itself received bad reviews, both the public and the critics raved about Ball's performance.*

before the show opened. Nonetheless, she forced herself to rehearse hard—seven days a week, from early until late. Ball was influenced during this period by a self-help book called *The Art of Selfishness*, which argued that society would improve if people looked out for their own best interests. She taped a message to her bathroom mirror—"Is this good for Lucy?"—and used it to make daily decisions.

Wildcat opened on Broadway in December 1960. Reviews were poor, the consensus being that Ball was wonderful but that the show was mediocre. Typical of the critical response was the comment of the *New York Times*: "Everybody wanted to love Lucille Ball, but her show didn't make it easy."[89]

The public, again, felt differently. Audiences loved Ball's performance as the boisterous Wildy Jackson. They clamored for encores of the show's biggest song, "Hey, Look Me Over." The shows regularly sold out, and adoring fans often stood up during curtain calls or waited at the stage door to yell "We love you, Lucy!"

GARY MORTON

Just before *Wildcat* opened, at a show-business restaurant called Danny's Hideaway, Ball was having dinner with a friend, agent Danny Welkes. Welkes spotted another friend, Gary Morton, and introduced him to Ball.

While leaning over her table to shake hands, Morton accidentally dipped the end of his tie in Ball's coffee cup. He was embarrassed, but she cheerfully gave him advice on how to clean it. The next day she found out where he lived and sent him three new ties. Soon the two were dating.

Born Morton Goldapper in the Bronx, Morton was tall, self-assured, and easygoing. A professional comic, he was a show-business veteran but had never achieved widespread fame. Ball liked, among other things, his sense of humor. "Before I met Gary," she recalled, "I hadn't laughed in years. I'd made other people laugh, but I hadn't laughed."[90]

Ball's friends were somewhat surprised that a star of her stature would be attracted to a "second banana" like Morton. They theorized, however, that she was grateful to have a reassuringly stable element in her life, a silver-haired father figure, after her years with the volatile and hard-living Arnaz. Another plus to the relationship, they realized, was that Ball's fame did not seem to intimidate Morton or make him jealous. Ball's friend, actress Shelley Winters, commented, "She realized she needed someone who wouldn't be clobbered too much by her success and who would take care of her."[91]

ANOTHER MARRIAGE

The stress of performing nightly on Broadway was by now genuinely wearing Ball down. She developed bursitis, strained her vocal cords, had to breathe from an oxygen tank between acts, and lost twenty-two pounds. It finally got to be too much, and the star reluctantly decided to close the show.

She was not eager to return to Los Angeles, the scene of her still-painful divorce,

Ball with her second husband Gary Morton, whom she married in November 1961.

but had no desire to stay in New York. Ball seriously considered moving to Switzerland and got as far as returning to California to sell her house and belongings. Once there, however, she could not give them up.

Together, Ball and Morton decided to move back to Los Angeles. First, they were married in New York City, in a quiet civil ceremony in November 1961. She told reporters at the time, "I look forward to a nice, quiet life."[92] The couple settled into Ball's Beverly Hills house. Her Hollywood friends were eager to meet the new spouse, and the two were invited to parties so often that Morton joked that he felt like a lamp being passed around for inspection. The couple was generally welcomed into Ball's Hollywood crowd—a

change from the final years of her first marriage, when Arnaz's drinking and erratic behavior had caused many of their friends to avoid them.

THE KIDS

Ball and Arnaz shared joint custody of Lucie and Desi Jr., but the children spent most of their time with Ball. Her years as a single mother served to intensify Ball's already difficult relationships with her children, and although her marriage to Morton stabilized many aspects of her life, these ties remained strained.

Arnaz adored his children, but even when the family was together, he had never found more than brief periods of time for them. Ball had always longed to have children, and she did her best to be a good mother; but her schedule was always busy and maternal instincts did not come naturally to her. As a result, since infancy Lucie and Desi Jr. had been raised primarily by Ball's mother, DeDe Peterson, and a nanny, Willie Mae Barker.

As the children grew older and asserted their independence, Ball often was short-tempered with them. She was also strict; she told a reporter, "In our home, it's school and homework; early to bed, and not so many dates, just on weekends. I know where [my children] are every minute."[93] Furthermore, she could be cruel, even when she did not mean to be. For instance, she frequently criticized them, privately and in public. Once, speaking to a reporter who published the remarks in a nationally syndicated piece, she verbally slapped Desi Jr. for failing his Spanish class, commenting that—considering who his father was—he should have done better.

TEENAGERS

Lucie and Desi Jr. got along well with Morton, who never tried to take on too much authority as a stepparent. Nonetheless, life was not easy for either of them, especially as they grew into their teen years. Eager to escape into independence from her critical mother, Lucie moved into her own apartment as soon as possible, when she turned eighteen. A year later she married an aspiring actor, but it was an unsuccessful union.

Desi Jr., meanwhile, generated scandalous gossip headlines even as an adolescent. He formed a pop trio with friends, Dean Martin Jr. and Billy Hinsche. Dino, Desi & Billy had a hit single and began touring when Desi Jr. was thirteen. His drug and alcohol problems, which he has battled all his life, began during this period. Desi Jr. also became involved with women, often ones older than he was. His mother tried to ignore these romantic adventures. When her son had an affair with the mother of one of his friends, however, Ball reportedly dumped her son's belongings on the offending woman's front lawn.

Desi Jr. also had a highly publicized romance with actress Patty Duke, who was six years older and, at the time, in the middle of a divorce. When she gave birth, she announced that Desi Jr. was the father of her baby. Ball reportedly did not believe Duke and refused to allow her or the baby in her house. Later Duke stated that the father was really another actor, John Astin, whom she later married.

BECOMING AN EXECUTIVE

Ball was still one of the main stockholders and directors of Desilu Productions. It was still the largest TV studio in the world; however, as Arnaz's drinking problems worsened, the studio's output had begun to drop. The once-bustling organization now turned out only a few hours of prime-time TV every week. Most of its income came from renting space to other companies.

On the advice of her longtime associates, Ball decided to buy out Arnaz's shares in the company. She did this reluctantly; always happiest on stage, she was not eager to be an executive. However, she felt that the purchase was the only way to keep Desilu from bankruptcy. In November 1962, therefore, Ball bought Arnaz out for an estimated $3 million. The comedian was now the company's main stockholder, president, and CEO. This made her the first woman to control a major Hollywood studio. She was self-deprecating, however, when reporters pointed out her unique status: "I had been vice-president in charge of dusting. Now I get to sweep up."[94]

She delegated much of the studio's day-to-day operation to others, including longtime associate Martin Leeds. Nonetheless, Ball's responsibilities were considerable, and they took up a great deal of her time

A family photo from 1965 shows Morton, Lucie, Ball, and Desi Jr. The distant relationship between Ball and her children intensified as they grew into teenagers.

Ball at an annual meeting of Desilu's stockholders. Ball bought out Arnaz's shares in the company and became president of Desilu Productions, Inc. in 1962.

and energy. By 1967 she grew tired of being both an actress and a studio executive. She hated the thought of giving up Desilu; she had always thought of it as a family operation. She could have retained ownership and turned the directorship over to others; however, her financial advisers convinced her that selling the studio was the best idea. Ball therefore sold Desilu to a multinational corporation, Gulf + Western, for an estimated $17 million.

MORE TELEVISION

Ball had continued to work with Desi Arnaz on several Desilu projects, even after the divorce. When she formed Lucille Ball Productions, a separate entity from Desilu, she made Morton vice president—but she also named Arnaz as director and producer of a new TV series she planned to star in. Relations among the three were understandably strained—while Ball hoped

(Left to right) Gale Gordon, guest star Vance, and Ball in a still from
Here's Lucy. *Vance was originally a regular cast member but left the show*
after a few seasons.

they would all get along, Arnaz mostly ignored or insulted Morton, and Morton
laughed it off. More than one observer has
noted that it was a strange and tense situation. Lucie Arnaz commented, "They
were trying to make it work, but it wasn't
healthy."[95]

The Lucille Ball Show, the new series, debuted in 1962. It cast the comedian as an
accident-prone widow with a teenage

daughter and a seven-year-old son. Two
longtime colleagues, Vivian Vance (as
Lucy's best friend) and Gale Gordon (as
Mr. Mooney, Lucy's banker), fleshed out
the primary cast. Dick Martin played the
star's neighbor, an airline pilot who was
around just enough to provide a hint of
romance. Lucie and Desi Jr. also appeared
on the show throughout its run (costarring
as the TV Lucy's children in later years).

Though the show was never as popular as *I Love Lucy*, Ball's return to television scored respectably high in the ratings. Under different names (*The Lucy Show* and *Here's Lucy*) and with variations in plot and casting, the show lasted until 1974. However, without the on-screen presence of Arnaz (or of Vivian Vance, who left the show after a few years), Ball was never able to recapture the magic of her early triumphs. The plots, critics complained, were often tired and trite. They also complained that Ball was unsuccessful at playing someone younger than she really was. The critic for *TV Guide* complained, "While we loved *I Love Lucy*, we can't even make friends with this show."[96]

SKIING ACCIDENT

During this period Ball enthusiastically took up a new hobby: skiing. In 1970 she bought three condominiums in the upscale ski resort of Snowmass, Colorado—enough room to accommodate herself, her children, her mother, and staff. The comedian liked Snowmass, in part, because she was able to appear in public without attracting a crowd. She also liked the cold mountain air, reminiscent of her childhood in Jamestown.

Unfortunately, in 1972 another skier struck Ball while she was on the slopes. The comedian fractured her leg in four places and required extensive surgery and nearly a year of rehabilitation. Even while recuperating, Ball refused to stop work entirely. Still in a wheelchair, she recorded twenty-four episodes of her show. Ball

eventually made a full recovery and remained remarkably limber for someone in her early sixties; she could still kick her leg to head height and touch her head to the ground while sitting cross-legged. Nonetheless, before she was fully recovered, Ball grew severely depressed, fearing she would never be able to work again. She credited Morton with helping her past this dark period: "Gary pulled me through. I never realized what a guy he is until that ordeal. He's somethin' else."[97]

SUCCESSIVE FLOPS

Meanwhile, Ball's TV series was beginning to slip in the ratings and was no longer even among the top twenty-five shows. She decided to end the series in 1974 after it became clear that her form of comedy was largely perceived as stale and old-fashioned.

For the last scene of the final episode of *Here's Lucy*, Ball made a wry comment on this perception. Her longtime sidekick Gale Gordon is the butt end of the oldest of slapstick jokes—getting hit in the face with a pie. His face covered with goop, Gordon looks straight at the camera and says with a sigh, "I *knew* it would end like this."[98]

In the years following the end of her regular series, Ball's other projects were, in general, poorly received. One especially notable disaster was her starring role in the film version of a hit Broadway musical, *Mame. The New Yorker's* influential reviewer Pauline Kael singled out for criticism Ball's ineffective attempt to play a much younger woman: "We in the audience are not thinking of fun, we're thinking of age and self-deception."[99]

A made-for-TV drama about a homeless woman, *Stone Pillow*, also flopped with audiences and critics. The handful of TV specials Ball made during this period, meanwhile, were only moderately successful. Of the pilots her company produced for shows not starring Ball, not a single one aired.

In 1986 the comedian attempted a final comeback in another sitcom, *Life with Lucy*. Despite the presence of several longtime collaborators, including Gale Gordon and the writing team of Madelyn Pugh and Bob Carroll, the show lasted only a humiliating eight weeks. Viewers were apparently uneasy watching a senior citizen hit her thumb with a hammer or trip on a rake—the sort of physical comedy, in other words,

Ball's performance in Mame *(pictured), a film version of the Broadway musical, was widely criticized.*

CLEANING HOUSES

In this passage, Ball reflects on how devastated she was by the humiliating cancellation of her final TV series, which lasted for only a handful of episodes. The quote is from Coyne Steven Sanders and Tom Gilbert's Desilu: The Story of Lucille Ball and Desi Arnaz:

"It was almost like losing my identity after all those years. It was a helluva jolt to find myself unemployed with nothing to do after more than twenty-five years of steady work. I think the fact that I love housework saved my sanity. The first thing I did was fire the household help that I'd had for twelve years. Then I set about to clean my house. It took me six months, but I cleaned everything. . . . When I got finished, I still didn't know what to do with myself, so I went over to Desi [Jr.]'s and cleaned *his* house."

with which Ball had once captured the nation's attention. The comedian was angry and hurt by the show's failure. "ABC's let me go," she tearfully told actress Ann Sothern, her longtime friend. "They don't want to see me as an old grandma. They want me as the Lucy I was."[100]

SMALLER CIRCLES

As the years progressed, Ball's social circle was growing smaller. She worked less and less, instead spent more time coddling her beloved poodles and playing games. Always an avid card and games player, Ball became obsessed in particular with backgammon. She played daily with friends and took part in weekly charity tournaments. She even hired a backgammon coach to help improve her game.

Her children, meanwhile, remained distant. Lucie Arnaz had married a second

time, to actor Laurence Luckinbill, settled in New York, and forged a successful career on Broadway. Desi Jr., meanwhile, married and remarried, entered various drug-rehab programs, and became closely involved with a quasi-religious organization called New Life Foundation.

Ball's social circle grew even smaller as longtime friends, family, and colleagues began to pass away. Her beloved mother DeDe died in 1977. Vivian Vance died in 1979. Then, in 1986 Desi Arnaz was diagnosed with lung cancer. The great love of Ball's life died late that year. Until the very end, Ball remained emotionally attached to him. Reporter Jim Bacon, who covered Hollywood for the Associated Press and knew both Arnaz and Ball, recalls, "Even after she'd married Gary, whenever she'd see me, she would always take me over to a corner and say, 'Have you heard from Desi lately?' She wanted to know how he was getting along. There was always that great, great love there."[101]

THE END

Ball's own health was failing as well. She felt that the making of *Stone Pillow*, which had been so physically punishing that she had become severely dehydrated and required a two-week hospital stay, was the final straw: "I *never* recovered from that."[102] In May 1988 Ball suffered a stroke while at home. After she was treated at Cedars-Sinai Hospital, a nurse moved into Ball's house. The nurse helped the comedian with her damaged speech and to regain the use of her partially paralyzed right side.

Ball made only a few public appearances after that. One was in March 1989, at the annual Academy Awards ceremony, when she and Bob Hope were invited to introduce a salute to young performers. She was lively and surprising—she came onstage in a daring black dress slit up the thigh—and the celebrities and power brokers in the audience gave her a huge and heartfelt ovation.

The end, however, was near. The following month Ball underwent emergency heart surgery for a damaged aorta. The medical emergency proved, if nothing else, that she had not been forgotten: while recovering in the hospital, Ball received five thousand cards of support a day. One was an eight-by-four-foot card

Lucie Arnaz and her husband Laurence Luckinbill. Although Ball longed to be close with her children, their relationship remained strained.

"LUCY WAS THE SHOW"

In 1986 Lucille Ball was presented with the most important of the many honors she received during her career: the Lifetime Achievement Award of the Kennedy Center Honors, the highest honor bestowed on Americans in the performing arts. The incident is reported in Coyne Steven Sanders and Tom Gilbert's *Desilu: The Story of Lucille Ball and Desi Arnaz*.

During the ceremony, actor Robert Stack read a statement prepared by her ex-husband, Desi Arnaz, before his death. As a tearful Ball listened, Stack read Arnaz's words, "The *New York Times* asked me to divide the credit for *I Love Lucy*'s success between the writers, the directors, and the cast. I told them, 'Give Lucy ninety percent of the credit—divide the other ten percent among the rest of us. Lucy *was* the show.'"

signed by four thousand residents of Louisiana.

The comedian's recovery from the surgery was brief. Lucille Ball died at age seventy-seven, of a heart attack, on April 26, 1989.

"THE LADY NEXT DOOR"

Tributes to Ball poured in from around the world, acknowledging her role as the greatest of the female comedians who pioneered television. Hosting one of the many television shows assembled to celebrate her life and honor her death, anchorman Dan Rather sounded a theme that typified the reaction of many. He

noted, "We lost a member of the family today, or maybe she was more like a good friend, the lady next door."[103]

According to Ball's wishes, the comedian had no public funeral. Instead, she was cremated and buried at Forest Lawn Cemetery in Los Angeles, next to her mother. Her children, their spouses, and Gary Morton were the only witnesses. A private memorial service—in the form of a casual picnic, as Ball had specified—was held shortly afterward.

The following month, large memorial gatherings were held in New York, Los Angeles, and Chicago. They took place on Monday, May 8, at nine in the evening, in honor of the woman who had once captivated America on that same day and hour.

Lucy's Legacy

"The sun never sets on Lucille Ball."
—Sammy Davis Jr.

Lucille Ball's work ethic never let her retire; her powerful talent and equally powerful need for recognition, meanwhile, kept her from fading away. Even when her performances were less than entirely successful, as with her later television shows and films, Ball was never far from the public eye during her lifetime.

Long after her death, Ball's work continues to be cherished by millions of fans. It serves, as well, as an inspiration for new generations of performers. The comedian's major achievements, particularly the groundbreaking *I Love Lucy* episodes, live on in reruns around the world.

THE MEMORIAL PICNIC

Jim Brochu, who befriended Ball near the end of her life, describes in this passage from his book Lucy in the Afternoon *the private memorial service held after her death:*

"Lucy left specific wishes as to what she wanted for a memorial service—a family picnic like the ones she remembered as a little girl in Jamestown. She left a list of what she wanted served, including ham, baked beans, potato salad, watermelon: all the things she remembered from her childhood. . . .

The picnic was held on Mother's Day at the old home of the late Robert Taylor in Mandeville Canyon. . . . The only person missing was Lucy. To have so many reminders of her around and not have her was making everyone misty. We were all laughing as we sat around the table telling Lucy stories, but the laughter was hollow. We all secretly hoped she would climb out on a window ledge and say, 'Ha-ha. Fooled you. I was just having fun.'"

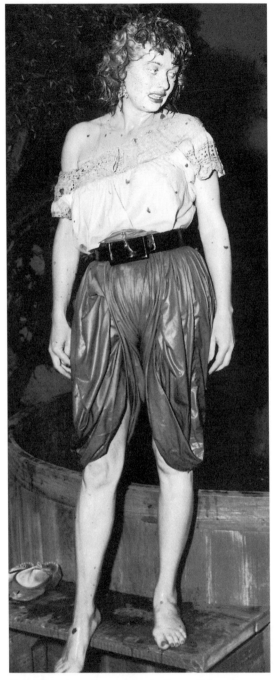

Ball after stomping grapes in the well-loved episode "Lucy's Italian Movie." I Love Lucy *reruns continue to entertain viewers around the world.*

Roughly eighty countries continue to regularly broadcast *Lucy* in syndication. Author Michael McClay asserts that since its first run, the show "has been playing almost continuously around the clock somewhere around the world. It's been estimated that *I Love Lucy* has been watched by over a billion people."[104]

By extension, the comedian who helped make television a habit, and the situation comedy into an art, lives on as well. Not just her work, but the comedian herself, seems to remain. At the time of Ball's death, her old friend Bob Hope said, "God has her now, but thanks to TV we'll have her forever."[105]

ROLE MODEL

Ball's legacy and story live on in many ways. For one thing, she serves as a role model for new generations of female television performers and personalities, who have been inspired to maintain creative and financial control of their work. This phenomenon was almost unheard of in Ball's day but is now commonplace. Mary Tyler Moore, Oprah Winfrey, and Roseanne are just three examples of female television performers who have successfully maintained control of their work by founding their own production companies. At the same time, Ball's comedic gifts continue to serve as role models for younger performers. Carol Burnett, Mary Tyler Moore, and Lily Tomlin are three of the many female comedians who have publicly stated that Ball was a primary influence on their work. Furthermore, during the 1950s and the original seasons of *I Love Lucy*, Ball's television persona served as an inspiration for many of her fans. For millions of women who tuned in on Monday nights, decades before the feminist movement took hold, Lucy Ricardo was a potent figure.

The premise of the show was that Ricky Ricardo, the man of the house, was in charge. He was the successful bandleader, the one who chuckled over and patronized his wife's crazy attempts to get into show business. The subtle joke, however, was that every minute of the show proved otherwise. Arnaz could sing and act well enough, but Ball was the performer that viewers could

not stop watching. Time and again, Lucy Ricardo would challenge and upstage Ricky. She was the one who was really in the spotlight, author Susan Faludi has observed, a situation that "was gratifying to so many women of that time who had to play the artificial role of second fiddle, the helpmate to their supposedly more competent, qualified husbands. It was a huge inside joke."[106]

CONTINUING INTEREST

Ball is still remembered fondly by fans in ways other than simply by watching her old shows on video or in reruns. Dozens

Ball and Morton with Mary Tyler Moore, one of the many comedians who credit Ball as a major influence and role model.

Ball's enduring appeal is witnessed not only in reruns of I Love Lucy, *but in the numerous Lucy books, websites, festivals, and even a museum.*

of Internet websites are devoted to her. Books about her, Arnaz, and her shows continue to appear at a steady rate. Her home town of Jamestown, New York, boasts a Lucy-Desi Museum and hosts an annual festival devoted to her.

In honor of the fiftieth anniversary of the debut of *I Love Lucy*, meanwhile, an elaborate museum exhibit began a four-year national tour in June 2001. The ex-

hibit features interactive games based on three of the show's most famous episodes —"Lucy's Italian Movie" (the grape-stomping episode), "Lucy Does a TV Commercial" (in which she accidentally gets drunk while tasting the product), and "Job Switching" (when Lucy and Ethel go to work in a candy factory).

Clearly, Lucy is still alive—and everyone still loves her.

Notes

Introduction: The First Lady of Television

1. Lucie Arnaz, introduction, Michael Mc-Clay, *I Love Lucy: The Complete Picture History of the Most Popular TV Show Ever*. New York: Warner Books, 1998, p. xii.

2. Quoted in Warren G. Harris, *Lucy & Desi*. New York: Simon & Schuster, 1991, p. 192.

3. Quoted in Coyne Steven Sanders and Tom Gilbert, *Desilu: The Story of Lucille Ball and Desi Arnaz*. New York: Morrow, 1993, p. 107.

4. Quoted in Susan Schindehette, "The Real Story of Desi and Lucy." *People Weekly*, February 18, 1991, p. 84.

5. Quoted in McClay, *I Love Lucy*, p. 114.

6. McClay, *I Love Lucy*, p. xii

7. Quoted in Harris, *Lucy & Desi*, p. 161.

8. Lucille Ball, *Love, Lucy*. New York: Putnam, 1996, p. 239.

9. Quoted in McClay, *I Love Lucy*, p. 114.

Chapter 1: The Young Lucy

10. Quoted in Kathleen Brady, *Lucille: The Life of Lucille Ball*, New York: Hyperion, 1994, p. 6.

11. Ball, *Love, Lucy*, p. 6.

12. Quoted in Harris, *Lucy & Desi*, p. 7.

13. Quoted in Joe Morella and Edward Z. Epstein, *Lucy: The Bittersweet Life of Lucille Ball*. Secaucus, NJ: Lyle Stuart, 1973, p. 4.

14. Ball, *Love, Lucy*, p. 22.

15. Quoted in Harris, *Lucy & Desi*, p. 22.

16. Quoted in Charles Higham, *Lucy: The Real Life of Lucille Ball*. New York: St. Martin's, 1986, p. 23.

17. Quoted in Brady, *Lucille*, p. 22.

18. Quoted in Brady, *Lucille*, p. 24.

19. Ball, *Love, Lucy*, p. 42.

20. Quoted in Sanders and Gilbert, *Desilu*, p. 206.

21. Quoted in Harris, *Lucy & Desi*, p. 35.

22. Ball, *Love, Lucy*, p. 70.

Chapter 2: "Queen of the B's"

23. Ball, *Love, Lucy*, p. 72.

24. Quoted in Brady, *Lucille*, p. 48.

25. Quoted in Brady, *Lucille*, p. 46.

26. Brady, *Lucille*, p. 49.

27. Quoted in Brady, *Lucille*, p. 59.

28. Quoted in Sanders and Gilbert, *Desilu*, p. 16.

29. Quoted in Brady, *Lucille*, p. 87.

30. Ball, *Love, Lucy*, p. 99.

31. Quoted in Higham, *Lucy*, p. 49.

Chapter 3: Lucy and Desi

32. Ball, *Love, Lucy*, p. 115.

33. Quoted in McClay, *I Love Lucy*, p. 10–11.

34. Brady, *Lucille*, p. 106.

35. Desi Arnaz, *A Book*. New York: Morrow, 1976, p. 113.

36. Ball, *Love, Lucy*, p. 146.

37. Arnaz, in McClay, *I Love Lucy*, p. xii.

38. Quoted in Brady, *Lucille*, p. 122.

39. Quoted in Brady, *Lucille*, p. 145.

40. Quoted in Sanders and Gilbert, *Desilu*, p. 26.

41. Quoted in Sanders and Gilbert, *Desilu*, p. 9.

42. Quoted in Brady, *Lucille*, p. 171.

43. Quoted in Sanders and Gilbert, *Desilu*, p. 28.

44. Quoted in Sanders and Gilbert, *Desilu*, p. 29.

Chapter 4: The Glory Years

45. Ball, *Love, Lucy*, p. 207.
46. Quoted in Higham, *Lucy*, p. 109.
47. Arnaz, *A Book*, p. 207.
48. Quoted in Sanders and Gilbert, *Desilu*, p. 41.
49. Ball, *Love, Lucy*, p. 204.
50. Quoted in Brady, *Lucille*, p. 181.
51. Quoted in *U.S. News & World Report*, "Lucy Has Grown Up a Lot" (interview), September 22, 1986, p. 80.
52. Ball, *Love, Lucy*, p. 205.
53. Quoted in Higham, *Lucy*, p. 123.
54. Quoted in Sanders and Gilbert, *Desilu*, p. 47.
55. McClay, *I Love Lucy*, p. 53.
56. Ball, *Love, Lucy*, p. 217.
57. Arnaz, *A Book*, p. 238.
58. Quoted in Sanders and Gilbert, *Desilu*, p. 68.
59. Quoted in Jim Brochu, *Lucy in the Afternoon*. New York: Morrow, 1990, p. 121.
60. Quoted in Brady, *Lucille*, p. 214.
61. Quoted in Harris, *Lucy & Desi*, p. 189.
62. Ball, *Love, Lucy*, p. 225.
63. Quoted in Arnaz, *A Book*, p. 248.
64. Quoted in Brady, *Lucille*, p. 218.
65. Quoted in Ball, *Love, Lucy*, p. 231.
66. Quoted in Higham, *Lucy*, p. 149.

Chapter 5: The Nonstop Star

67. Brady, *Lucille*, p. 202.
68. Quoted in Sanders and Gilbert, *Desilu*, p. 257.
69. Quoted in Brady, *Lucille*, p. 209.
70. Quoted in Sanders and Gilbert, *Desilu*, p. 50.
71. Arnaz, in McClay, *I Love Lucy*, p. xix.
72. Quoted in Sanders and Gilbert, *Desilu*, p. 48.
73. Quoted in Sanders and Gilbert, *Desilu*, p. 25.
74. Quoted in Harris, *Lucy & Desi*, pp. 120–21.
75. Quoted in Brady, *Lucille*, p. 244.
76. Quoted in Brochu, *Lucy in the Afternoon*, p. 101.
77. Quoted in Brady, *Lucille*, p. 207.
78. Quoted in Sanders and Gilbert, *Desilu*, p. 111.
79. Quoted in Sanders and Gilbert, *Desilu*, p. 154.
80. Arnaz, in McClay, *I Love Lucy*, p. xx.
81. Quoted in Schindehette, "The Real Story of Desi and Lucy," p. 84.
82. Quoted in Brady, *Lucille*, p. 225.
83. Ball, *Love, Lucy*, p. 257.
84. Ball, *Love, Lucy*, p. 260.
85. Quoted in Brady, *Lucille*, p. 261.

Chapter 6: The Marriage Ends, but the Shows Go On

86. Quoted in Brady, *Lucille*, p. 262.
87. Quoted in Sanders and Gilbert, *Desilu*, p. 207.
88. Quoted in Sanders and Gilbert, *Desilu*, p. 211.
89. Quoted in Harris, *Lucy & Desi*, p. 263.
90. Quoted in Sanders and Gilbert, *Desilu*, p. 216.
91. Quoted in Schindehette, "The Real Story of Desi and Lucy," p. 84.
92. Quoted in Brady, *Lucille*, p. 274.
93. Quoted in Higham, *Lucy*, p. 208.
94. Quoted in Brady, *Lucille*, p. 283.
95. Quoted in Beth Johnson, "Desilu's Redhead Honcho: Lucille Ball Took Charge of

Her Famed TV Studio 34 Years Ago," *Entertainment Weekly*, November 15, 1996, p. 92.

96. Quoted in Harris, *Lucy & Desi*, p. 288.

97. Quoted in Sanders and Gilbert, *Desilu*, p. 337.

98. Quoted in Harris, *Lucy & Desi*, p. 300.

99. Quoted in Brady, *Lucille*, p. 324.

100. Quoted in Harris, *Lucy & Desi*, p. 321.

101. Quoted in Schindehette, "The Real Story of Desi and Lucy," p. 84.

102. Quoted in Brochu, *Lucy in the Afternoon*, p. 26.

103. Quoted in Sanders and Gilbert, *Desilu*, p. 360.

Epilogue: Lucy's Legacy

104. McClay, *I Love Lucy*, p. xi.

105. Quoted in Brian D. Johnson, "They All Loved Lucy: Lucille Ball, the Sitcom Queen, Dies at 77," *Maclean's*, May 8, 1989, p. 61.

106. Quoted in Steve Daly, "The 100 Greatest Entertainers: No. 9, Lucille Ball." *Entertainment Weekly*, November 1, 1999, p. 52.

For Further Reading

Bart Andrews, *Loving Lucy: An Illustrated Tribute to Lucille Ball.* New York: St. Martin's, 1980. A book with brief biographical sketches and many photographs, poorly reproduced.

Katherine E. Krohn, *Lucille Ball: Pioneer of Comedy.* Minneapolis: Lerner, 1992. A brief book for younger readers.

Michael McClay, with an introduction by Lucie Arnaz, *I Love Lucy: The Complete Picture History of the Most Popular TV Show Ever.* New York: Warner Books, 1998. A large picture book with biographical data, excellent photos, and detailed synopses of the most famous *I Love Lucy* episodes, written by a former Desilu executive (who is also the son of one of Ball's longtime publicity agents).

Works Consulted

Books

Desi Arnaz, *A Book.* New York: Morrow, 1976. The memoirs of Lucille Ball's former husband and onstage partner.

Lucille Ball, *Love, Lucy.* New York: Putnam, 1996. A memoir written in 1964 but not published until after Ball's death.

Kathleen Brady, *Lucille: The Life of Lucille Ball.* New York: Hyperion, 1994. Well-researched and evenhanded, this is the best biography to date of the actress.

Jim Brochu, *Lucy in the Afternoon.* New York: Morrow, 1990. A memoir by a young actor who befriended Ball late in her life.

Warren G. Harris, *Lucy & Desi.* New York: Simon & Schuster, 1991. A dual biography with an emphasis on the less savory aspects of its subjects' lives, marred by dubious reconstructed dialogue.

Charles Higham, *Lucy: The Real Life of Lucille Ball.* New York: St. Martin's, 1986. A well-done book by a biographer of Hollywood celebrities.

Joe Morella and Edward Z. Epstein, *Lucy: The Bittersweet Life of Lucille Ball.* Secaucus, NJ: Lyle Stuart, 1973. A somewhat dubious early biography.

Coyne Steven Sanders and Tom Gilbert, *Desilu: The Story of Lucille Ball and Desi Arnaz.* New York: Morrow, 1993. This book by two veteran entertainment-industry reporters focuses on the rise and fall of Desilu Productions, but suffers from a lack of footnotes or other attribution.

Periodicals

Steve Daly, "The 100 Greatest Entertainers: No. 9, Lucille Ball," *Entertainment Weekly,* November 1, 1999, p. 52.

William A. Henry III, "A Zany Red-headed Everywoman: Lucille Ball: 1911–1989," *Time,* May 8, 1989, p. 101.

Beth Johnson, "Desilu's Redhead Honcho: Lucille Ball Took Charge of Her Famed TV Studio 34 Years Ago," *Entertainment Weekly,* November 15, 1996, p. 92.

Brian D. Johnson, "They All Loved Lucy: Lucille Ball, the Sitcom Queen, Dies at 77," *Maclean's,* May 8, 1989, p. 61.

Susan Schindehette, "The Real Story of Desi and Lucy." *People Weekly,* February 18, 1991, p. 84.

U.S. News & World Report, "Lucy Has Grown Up a Lot," (interview), September 22, 1986, p. 80.

Index

Picture Credits

Cover photo: The Kobal Collection

©Bettmann/CORBIS, 24, 45, 68, 78, 89

Hulton/Archive by Getty Images, 14, 31, 58, 88, 94

Library of Congress, 10, 27, 29, 76

Photofest, 13, 16, 22, 28, 33 (both), 34, 36, 37, 39, 40, 43, 47, 49, 51, 52, 57, 59, 60, 63, 65, 66, 71, 72, 74, 83, 84, 86, 90, 92, 97, 98, 99

©Underwood & Underwood/CORBIS, 19, 20, 46

©Oscar White/CORBIS, 80

About the Author

Adam Woog, the author of more than thirty books for adults, young adults, and children, has a special interest in twentieth-century American pop culture. Among his other books for Lucent are volumes on Harry Houdini, Elvis Presley, Steven Spielberg, George Lucas, and the history of rock and roll. He lives with his wife and daughter in his hometown of Seattle.